The

CHURCH
and AGE *of*
the
REFORMATIONS
(1350–1650)

"The intricate interplay of religion and politics was never more dramatic than in the age of the Reformation. But too often the era is presented as though the Protestant reformers were the heroes. However, in a very real way, they failed to reform the Church and instead took the easier way out of creating separate ecclesial bodies with the leaders of their movements humbly offering themselves up to be the popes of their particular versions of utopian Christianity! The true heroes of the Reformation are those who remained in the Church while reforming her from within. Joseph and Barbara Stuart's book is a very-much-needed treatment of those often unsung heroes. Anyone who is inclined (or assigned) to read about the Protestant Reformation in any books written from the Protestant perspective owes it to themselves—for the sake of balance—to read this book first. It is an indispensable introduction to the Reformation era that puts all other treatments in their proper perspective. This book is an eloquent reminder that it is always more important for our religion to reform us, rather than the other way around, and that, in and of itself, schism and revolution are not reform."

James L. Papandrea
Author of *The Early Church* in the Reclaiming Catholic History series

"It is hard to imagine an event that has shaped the modern world more than the Reformation. Joseph and Barbara Stuart serve as able guides through its complexities by exploring its causes, major figures and events, and aftermath. Their book is fresh and compelling, leading us to revisit the past in order to bring its lessons into the present."

R. Jared Staudt
Associate superintendent for mission and formation for the Archdiocese of Denver
Visiting associate professor at the Augustine Institute

"As a veteran Catholic educator and historian, I have witnessed that perhaps no greater source of confusion and misunderstanding exists than the Reformation era. However, it need not be so. This phenomenal yet accessible text by Joseph and Barbara Stuart will equip Catholics—and anyone of good will from any faith tradition—to more effectively understand what really happened during the controversial period. Readers will also be pleasantly surprised that they can likewise better grasp the several 'lowercase r' reforms that redirected Catholic practices back to the holiness, righteousness, and virtue that Christ intended when he founded the Church as per Matthew 16:18."

Justin McClain
Catholic author and teacher

The CHURCH *and the* AGE *of* REFORMATIONS
(1350–1650)

*Martin Luther, the Renaissance,
and the Council of Trent*

JOSEPH T. STUART AND BARBARA A. STUART

Series Editor, Mike Aquilina

AVE MARIA PRESS AVE Notre Dame, Indiana

⫯ RECLAIMING CATHOLIC HISTORY ⫰

The history of the Catholic Church is often clouded by myth, misinformation, and missing pieces. Today there is a renewed interest in recovering the true history of the Church, correcting the record in the wake of centuries of half-truths and noble lies. Books in the Reclaiming Catholic History series, edited by Mike Aquilina and written by leading authors and historians, bring Church history to life, debunking the myths one era at a time.

Founded in 1865, Ave Maria Press is a ministry of the United States Province of Holy Cross.

www.avemariapress.com

Paperback: ISBN-13 978-1-64680-033-9

E-book: ISBN-13 978-1-64680-034-6

Cover images © Getty Images.

Cover and text design by Andy Wagoner.

Printed and bound in the United States of America.

Library of Congress Cataloging-in-Publication Data
Names: Stuart, Joseph, author. | Stuart, Barbara A., author.
Title: The Church and the age of reformations (1350-1650) : Martin Luther, the Renaissance, and the Council of Trent / Joseph and Barbara Stuart.
Description: Notre Dame, Indiana : Ave Maria Press, [2021] | Series: Reclaiming Catholic history | Includes bibliographical references and index. | Summary: "Joseph and Barbara Stuart highlight the watershed events of the reformation period (including the Protestant schism and Council of Trent), profile the main Catholic and Protestant figures such as Martin Luther and Desiderius Erasmus, and give readers the guidance they need to understand the deeper context and consequences of these tumultuous centuries"-- Provided by publisher.
Identifiers: LCCN 2021048149 (print) | LCCN 2021048150 (ebook) | ISBN 9781646800339 (paperback) | ISBN 9781646800346 (ebook)
Subjects: LCSH: Church history--Middle Ages, 600-1500. | Reformation. | Church history--16th century. | Church history--17th century.
Classification: LCC BR145.3 .S78 2021 (print) | LCC BR145.3 (ebook) | DDC 270.5--dc23/eng/20211116
LC record available at https://lccn.loc.gov/2021048149
LC ebook record available at https://lccn.loc.gov/2021048150

TO MY PARENTS,
FAE AND EDWARD STUART

because of them, the "woman with the beautiful face" found me and taught me. —JS

TO MY MOM AND DAD,
LAURA AND JAMES FRANK

none of this is possible without you. Thank you. —BS

Contents

⫸ RECLAIMING CATHOLIC HISTORY ⫷
Series Introduction

"History is bunk," said the inventor Henry Ford. And he's not the only cynic to venture judgment. As long as people have been fighting wars and writing books, critics have been there to grumble because "history is what's written by the winners."

Since history has so often been corrupted by political motives, historians in recent centuries have labored to "purify" history and make it a bare science. From now on, they declared, history should record only facts, without any personal interpretation, without moralizing, and without favoring any perspective at all.

It sounds like a good idea. We all want to know the facts. The problem is that it's just not possible. We cannot record history the way we tabulate results of a laboratory experiment. Why not? Because we cannot possibly record all the factors that influence a single person's actions—his genetic makeup, the personalities of his parents, the circumstances of his upbringing, the climate in his native land, the state of the economy, the anxieties of his neighbors, the popular superstitions of his time, his chronic indigestion, the weather on a particular day, the secret longings of his heart.

For any action taken in history, there is simply too much material to record, and there is so much more we do not know and can never know. Even if we were to collect data scrupulously and voluminously, we would still need to assign it relative importance. After all, was the climate more important than his genetic makeup?

But once you begin to select certain facts and leave others out—and once you begin to emphasize some details over others—you have begun to impose your own perspective, your interpretation, and your idea of the story.

Still, there is no other way to practice history honestly. When we read, or teach, or write history, we are discerning a story line. We are saying that certain events are directly related to other events. We say that events proceed in a particular manner until they reach a particular end, and that they resolve themselves in a particular way.

Every historian has to find the principle that makes sense of those events. Some choose economics, saying that all human decisions are based on the poverty or prosperity of nations and neighborhoods, the comfort or needs of a given person or population. Other historians see history as a succession of wars and diplomatic maneuvers. But if you see history this way, you are not practicing a pure science. You are using an interpretive key that you've chosen from many possibilities, but which is no less arbitrary than the one chosen in olden days, when the victors wrote the history. If you choose wars or economics, you are admitting a certain belief: that what matters most is power, wealth, and pleasure in this world. In doing so, you must assign a lesser role, for example, to the arts, to family life, and to religion.

But if there is a God—and most people believe there is—then God's view of things should not be merely incidental or personal. God's outlook should define objectivity. God's view should provide the objective meaning of history.

So how do we get God's view of history? Who can scale the heavens to bring God down? We can't, of course. But since God chose to come down and reveal himself and his purposes to us, we might be able to find what the Greek historians and philosophers despaired of ever finding—that is, the basis for a universal history.

The pagans knew that they could not have a science without universal principles. But universal principles were elusive because no one could transcend his own culture—and no one dared to question the rightness of the regime.

Not until the Bible do we encounter histories written by historical losers. God's people were regularly defeated, enslaved, oppressed, occupied, and exiled. Yet they told their story honestly, because they held themselves—and their historians—to a higher judgment, higher even than the king or the forces of the market. They looked at history in terms of God's judgment, blessings, curses, and mercy. This became their principle of selection and interpretation of events. It didn't matter so much whether the story flattered the king or the victorious armies.

The Bible's human authors saw history in terms of covenant. In the ancient world, a covenant was the sacred and legal way that people created a family bond. Marriage was a covenant, and adoption was a covenant. And God's relationship with his people was always based on a covenant.

God's plan for the kingdom of heaven uses the kingdoms of earth. And these kingdoms are engaged by God and evangelized for his purpose. Providence harnesses the road system and the political system of the Roman Empire, and puts it all to use to advance the Gospel. Yet Rome, too, came in for divine judgment. If God did not spare the holy city of Jerusalem, then neither would Rome be exempted.

And so the pattern continued through all the subsequent thousands of years—through the rise and fall of the Byzantine Empire, the European empires, and into the new world order that exists for our own fleeting moment.

There's a danger, of course, in trying to discern God's perspective. We run the risk of moralizing, presuming too much, or playing the prophet. There's always a danger, too, of identifying God with one "side" or another in a given war or rivalry. Christian history, at its best, transcends these problems. We can recognize that even when pagan Persia was the most vehement enemy of Christian Byzantium, the tiny Christian minority in Persia was practicing the most pure and refined Christianity the world has seen. When God uses imperial structures to advance the Gospel, the imperial structures have no monopoly on God.

It takes a subtle, discerning, and modest hand to write truly Christian history. In studying world events, a Christian historian must strive to see God's fatherly plan for the whole human race and how it has unfolded since the first Pentecost.

Christian history tells the story not of an empire, nor of a culture, but of a family. And it is a story, not a scientific treatise. In many languages, the connection is clear. In Spanish, Portuguese, Italian, and German, for example, the same word is used for "history" as for "story": *historia, história, storia, Geschichte*. In English we can lose sight of this and teach history as a succession of dates to be memorized and maps to be drawn. The timelines and atlases are certainly important, but they don't communicate to ordinary people why they should want to read history. Jacques Barzun complained, almost a half century ago, that history had fallen out of usefulness for ordinary people and was little read. It had fragmented into overspecialized microdisciplines, with off-putting names like "psychohistory" and "quantohistory."

The authors in this series strive to communicate history in a way that's accessible and even entertaining. They see history as true stories well told. They don't fear humor or pathos as threats to their trustworthiness. They are unabashed about their chosen perspective, but they are neither producing propaganda nor trashing tradition. The sins and errors of Christians (even Christian saints) are an important part of the grand narrative.

The Catholic Church's story is our inheritance, our legacy, our pride and joy, and our cautionary tale. We ignore the past at our peril. We cannot see the present clearly without a deep sense of Christian history.

Mike Aquilina
Reclaiming Catholic History Series Editor

Chronology of *The Church and the Age of Reformations (1350–1650)*

1309–1376	The Avignon Papacy occurs, in which seven successive popes reside in Avignon rather than Rome.
1330	John Wycliffe, founder of the Lollard movement, is born in England
1340	Gerard Groote, founder of the Brothers and Sisters of the Common Life, is born in the Netherlands
1347	St. Catherine of Siena, mystic and Doctor of the Church, is born in Italy
1347–1351	The Black Death kills 200 million people throughout Eurasia
1378–1417	The Great Schism splits the papacy into separate political factions
1414–1418	Council of Constance
1436	Francisco Jiménez de Cisneros is born in Spain, later to become a cardinal and advisor to Queen Isabella of Castille
1439	The printing press is invented in Germany by Johannes Gutenberg
1447	St. Catherine of Genoa, mystic and patron of the poor, is born in Italy
1452	Girolamo Savonarola, a popular Dominican preacher, is born in Italy

1466	Humanist writer Desiderius Erasmus is born in Rotterdam
1469	Niccolò Machiavelli, author of *The Prince*, is born in Italy
1483	Martin Luther, famous German Protestant reformer, is born in Germany
1484	Albrecht Zwingli, leader of the Reform church in Zurich, is born in Switzerland
1486	Johann Eck, a German theological rival to Luther, is born; Andreas Karlstadt is born in Wittenberg
1491	St. Ignatius of Loyola is born in Spain
1492	Christopher Columbus sails to the "New World" under the direction of the Spanish crown
1498	Felix Manz, Anabaptist leader and martyr of the Radical Reformation, is born in Zurich
1506	Peter Faber, cofounder of the Society of Jesus, is born in France
1509	Henry VIII becomes King of England; John Calvin is born in France
1512	Michelangelo's Sistine Chapel is completed, under the patronage of Pope Leo X
1512–1517	Fifth Lateran Council called to restore peace between Catholic leaders and affirm papal authority, but little was done to implement it
1514	Oratory of Divine Love founded in Rome after the teachings of St. Catherine of Genoa
1515	St. Philip Neri is born in Florence; he will go on to found several lay religious groups

1517	Martin Luther publishes the *Ninety-Five Theses* in Wittenberg, triggering the beginning of the Protestant Reformations
1521	Diet of Worms called by Emperor Charles V; St. Peter Canisius born in the Netherlands
1522	Martin Luther's German edition of the New Testament is published
1524–1525	German Peasants' War
1525–1528	Capuchin order founded; Poor Clares in Nuremberg fight against Protestantization of the convent
1529	Siege of Vienna initiated by the Ottoman Turks
1534	Anabaptist rebellion begins in Münster, Germany; Act of Supremacy initiated by Henry VIII
1535	Thomas More is executed in England; Ursuline order founded by St. Angela Merici
1538	St. Charles Borromeo, cardinal and leader of the Catholic Reformation, born in Italy
1540	The Society of Jesus (Jesuit order) is founded in Paris by Ignatius of Loyola and his six companions
1541	Genevan Consistory instituted as part of the implementation of John Calvin's *Ecclesiastical Ordinances*
1542	Spanish mystic St. John of the Cross is born; Roman Inquisition begins
1545–1563	The Council of Trent, defining the Church's position in the Catholic Reformation
1549	Prayer Book Rebellion occurs in England following the institution of the *Book of Common Prayer*

1553–1558   Catholic Queen Mary of England reigns, executing many English Protestants

1555   Peace of Augsburg permits Christian rulers to choose either Catholicism or Lutheranism as their state religion

1559   Elizabeth I's Act of Uniformity prohibits the celebration of the Catholic mass in England; she executes many Catholics; Protestant books are banned in Rome; St. Lawrence of Brindisi is born in Italy

1566–1572   Reign of Pope Pius V

1567   St. Francis de Sales, bishop of Geneva, is born in France

1571   The Thirty-Nine Articles finalize the teachings of the Church of England; Turks defeated at the Battle of Lepanto; Italian painter Caravaggio born in Milan

1572   St. Bartholomew's Day Massacre in France kills thousands of Protestants

1575   Thomas Helwys, cofounder of the Baptists, is born in England

1586   Church of the Gesù, first Baroque church, is built in Rome; St. Margaret Clitherow martyred for hiding Catholic priests in her English home

1598   The Edict of Nantes grants Huguenots religious freedom in France

1616–1633   The Galileo affair demonstrates how the defensive posture of many Catholic leaders concerning biblical interpretation could cause new problems

1618–1648   Thirty Years' War initially fought between Catholic and Protestant troops in Central Europe continues, killing several million people

1622   Pope Gregory XV canonizes Ignatius of Loyola, Teresa of
            Ávila, Philip Neri, and Francis Xavier; initiates the Con-
            gregation for the Propagation of the Faith to direct mis-
            sionary activities

1626   New St. Peter's Basilica completed in Rome

1642–1651   Religious differences are a major factor in the English Civil
            War fought between supporters of King Charles I and Par-
            liament that killed several hundred thousand people across
            the British Isles

MARK

OLY
MAN
PIRE

● Zwickau

● Nuremberg
Augsburg

rich

Vienna
●

● Trent

VENICE

Milan

enoa

Florence
●

PAPAL STATES

Rome
●

OTTOMAN EMPIRE

MEDITERRANEAN SEA

Introduction

Why did everyone ignore Egidio da Viterbo? He was one of the most renowned scholars and public speakers in Italy when he addressed the Fifth Lateran Council in 1512. His famous opening sermon warned of the "greedy desire for human things" that needed to yield to "love of divine things" or "it is all over with Christendom, all over with religion." When had there even been greater neglect of the sacred among the people of any age? he asked earnestly. Unbridled living afflicted the heart of the Church with wounds so great there was a desperate need for reform. Egidio's prestigious audience in the basilica of St. John Lateran was moved to tears, praised the oration, and talked for five years. They promulgated documents but did nothing.

Egidio was the general of the Augustinian Order who had labored for years for reform both inside and outside his order. He even interacted with the young Augustinian monk Martin Luther when he visited Rome in the winter of 1510 concerning Egidio's plans for reform, as well as Girolamo Seripando, the great Augustinian theologian at the future Council of Trent. What a confluence of different ideas of reform in these men!

The Fifth Lateran Council ended in March 1517. Immediately afterward, Luigi d'Aragona, one of the cardinals at the council responsible for carrying out reform, passed through the pleasant city of Trent into Germany on an expensive tour with his large entourage of officials and servants. He seemed more interested in buying fine watches and meeting with rich men than in reform. Later that year, Luther published his *Ninety-Five Theses* attacking Church corruption. Egidio had told the Council Fathers gathered in 1512 that "men must be changed by religion, not religion by men."[1] This was Egidio's idea of reform. Nevertheless, in the name of reform, Luther eventually broke from the Church and changed religion in ways he never imagined or intended, launching a religious revolution that altered the course of modern history.

How did such a result come about, especially when there were so many examples of successful reform within the Church over the centuries? The Council of Jerusalem in AD 50, for example, and the Cluniac Reform and the Fourth Lateran Council in the Middle Ages, advanced reform and at the same time maintained the unity of the Church. Why did this not happen in the 1500s? Reform had long been central to Christian life. So why did mutually exclusive ideas of reform arise in the Age of Reformations, gain so many supporters, and cause so much division? What went wrong in the late Middle Ages? And what were the consequences of the new situation pitting Catholics against Protestants and Protestants against each other? Also, what principles guided Catholic reformers and saints who continued to maintain unity with the Church during this time of crisis? These are the questions this book addresses, covering the years 1350–1650.

Catholics finally took up the widespread call for reform in a systematic way at the Council of Trent (1545–1563), the very city the ineffectual Luigi d'Aragona passed through on his tour. This council was so important and so comprehensive that another like it was not needed for four hundred years—until Vatican Council II (1962–1965). Even then, Vatican II was more about "updating" the faith than reform of systematic abuses. The Age of Reformations resulted in the fragmenting of Western Christianity but also in new forms of Christian life and culture. The simple argument of this book is that the Church in the Age of Reformations provides a case study in the principles of true reform and in the challenging conditions of the time that obscured them.

While most Christians would agree that "true reform is a matter of regaining and maintaining the true image of Christ, and the true reformer is the one who most fully expresses the image of Christ in all facets of life,"[2] what does that mean at the institutional level? That is where Christians have disagreed with each other ever since the Age of Reformations.

It was just before Vatican II that the French Dominican Yves Congar (1904–1995) formulated four principles by which true institutional reform could be accomplished from the Catholic perspective without producing a schism (division in the Church). First, true reform is rooted in charity and pastoral concerns. Intellectual effort must not neglect the "concrete reality and the given quality" of the Church as she exists within history.

Second, true reform must remain in communion with the whole body of the Church as animated by the Holy Spirit. Only in this way can one have access to all revealed truth. The spirit of unity must be present from the center to the periphery of a debate or of a community. Typically, it is the "periphery" (theologians, religious orders, prophetic personalities, laypeople) that pushes reform while the center (the Church hierarchy) sees itself as the authoritative preserver of tradition. The periphery wants things to change while the center wants them to stay the same. There is a creative tension between authority and reform that is not bad.

Third, patience is needed to avoid schism, even though reformers are often restless. Patience in this sense is not the mere endurance of time and delays. It is spiritual docility, Congar wrote, "a mistrust of self, holding back when tempted by simple, abrupt solutions or by extremes of 'all or nothing.'"

Fourth, reform leading to genuine renewal and not to schism involves loyalty to the principle of tradition. This is not static changelessness. The historian Jaroslav Pelikan described tradition as the "living faith of the dead" and the "perpetuation of a changing, developing identity." In this spirit, one does not start with enthusiasm for new ideas and then try to change the Church accordingly. Rather, one loves the Church *as she is* and helps her adapt to new ideas and conditions, Congar thought.[3]

It would be unfair to judge sixteenth-century reformers entirely by later formulations like this. In fact, it was precisely the struggles and experiences of these reformers that now gives clarity to Congar's principles through hindsight. And yet, during the Age of Reformations and even before, some Christians (especially the saints) did have a sense for these principles of true reform, as we will see. For many people at the time, however, these principles were not clear, and the direction of true reform was uncertain.

In the Age of Reformations, numerous challenges converged to confuse people about true reform. The new literate culture emerging due to the invention of the printing press around 1439 seemed to make *texts* more authoritative than *living people* such as wise elders or Church leaders. This contributed to a catechetical crisis. In addition, the resurgence of a kind of spiritualism in the Renaissance cast doubt on the material world as a vehicle of spiritual reality, undermining the sacraments.

A new view of history emerged that negated the very idea of tradition. It characterized the "Middle Ages" as dark and unimportant, and the classical era of early Christianity as the ideal pattern for Christian life. All subsequent history was decline. This broke historical continuity and development of doctrine. It also injected a dose of utopianism into the intellectual life of the age by giving rise to unrealistic hopes for Christians to reform by purging all corruption from among themselves and society.

Because the gap between Christian ideals and the messiness of real life seemed wider than ever and corruption clearly remained in the old Church, that seemed to prove the need to "start over." Several new Christian churches emerged. The resulting conflict of theological voices calling for divergent ideas of reform constituted one of the central dramas of the age.

Then there was the political temptation. Zealous Catholic and Protestant reformers often aspired to governmental control of society. This created militant religious ideologies seeking to force reform in ways that easily betrayed Christian charity and respect for religious freedom. The perceived need to seek political solutions created huge challenges for authentic reform in the long run.

Finally, apocalypticism and impatience with the "ungodly" led to dreams of social revolution and violence. This was the temptation of pride in reformers, wishing God would show himself powerful, put down evil, and create a better world—through their help!

All these challenges obscured the principles Congar identified—charity, unity, patience, and tradition—that have helped secure true reform without schism in the history of the Church. These difficulties made up the context in which the singular contribution of saints like Teresa of Ávila and Charles Borromeo stood out. Powerful and innovative reformers such as these two saints maintained their allegiance to the principle of reform *and* to the principle of authority that safeguarded the unity of the Church. They demonstrated charity and patience toward those around them, and they fomented change within their commitment to tradition. "She [the Church] moves forward mysteriously as a kind of oligarchy of the influence of the saints. . . . The Church has followed her saints," one scholar wrote.[4] That was certainly true in the Age of Reformations.

We approach our subject from the perspectives of both history and theology, our fields of expertise. That is because more than theological differences came into play during the Age of Reformations. Human spiritual freedom is not the freedom of pure spirits but rather the difficult freedom of people embedded in history and influenced by events outside their control. If one was born in 1550 in Spain, for example, one was likely to be a Catholic; if in Denmark, then a Lutheran. The religious choices of individuals were largely made for them by previous generations. The historian Christopher Dawson wrote that the decisions of one person—an apostle or a heresiarch, a king or a statesman—affected the spiritual destinies of millions of ordinary people. It is no less a mistake for the theologian to ignore historical context than it is for the historian to miss the "reality and the creative power of religious truth."[5]

Chapter 1

Reform in the Late Middle Ages

The Woman with the Beautiful Face

One fine May morning, weary of walking, the poet William Langland (ca. 1330–ca. 1400) fell asleep on an English hillside beside a babbling brook. He dreamed of a great mountain, a murky valley, and a field full of people. He saw all manner of men and women, including nobles and villagers. Down from the castle on the mountain came a lovely lady in linen garments. "Son, do you sleep?" she asked him. "Do you see this people, how busy they are about the meadow?" Langland observed them again and waited for the lady to continue. "Most of the men who move in this meadow have their worship in this world and wish no better," she said. "No heaven but here holds their fancy." Langland did know what to say. "I was afraid of her face," he wrote, "for all her beauty."

Langland then managed to mumble, "Mercy, Madam, what is your meaning?" She told him the castle on the mountain was Truth's dwelling. "Would that you worked as his word teaches!" she exclaimed. He who lives in the castle is the father of faith, she told him, and fashioned you wholly. The beautiful lady spoke to him at length in words weighted with the wisdom of scripture. He wondered who she was who taught him so mildly.

"I am Holy Church," she said, "and you should know me. I first found you. My faith I taught you."

1

Langland kissed the ground and asked her to pray for him a sinner. "Teach me to believe in Christ," he begged. "Tell me of no treasure, but teach me only how I may save my soul, O sainted Lady!"[1]

So begins *The Vision of Piers Plowman*, one of the greatest poems of medieval England. It emerged from the heart of a Catholic people and was well known in its day. The author, William Langland, was a married layman in minor orders—or a "liturgical minister" in today's terminology. He earned his living in London by praying and singing psalms for the wealthy.

Since the best part of the Church is in heaven and is thereby holy, Langland portrayed it as a beautiful woman in the poem. But "Holy Church" was not always so holy on earth. The figure of the "plowman" in Langland's work represented the man of hardworking, Christlike simplicity seeking the path of salvation in a corrupt age, full of greed and lust and sloth—even among high churchmen. There was a wide gap between Christian ideals and actual ways of life, Langland observed, marring the Church's beauty on earth. It was obvious to him that the Antichrist and his army had infiltrated the highest reaches. His poem was a cry for reform.

Infiltrated

The medieval period constituted the turning point in the two-thousand-year story of reform of the Church. The idea of *personal reform* through the Holy Spirit, common among the Church Fathers, expanded to include the whole Church. Not only should individuals allow their hearts to be converted and monasteries reform by returning to the purity of their original rules, but also the papacy itself should lead the way for the Church as a whole *in capite et in membris* (in head and members). This idea of reform from top to bottom (either from the papacy or from councils) fired the imagination of the late Middle Ages among all those who wanted to take the gospel of Christ seriously. However, reform could also operate from the bottom up.

The zeal to reform was often accompanied by the zeal to criticize an existing state of affairs and demand change. There was much to criticize in the late medieval Church. The papacy was mired in financial and political problems. The pope even fled Rome due to political instability. This inaugurated the Avignon Papacy from 1309 to 1376 in France. After the pope returned to Rome, several men claimed to be pope. This created the Great Western Schism from 1378 to 1417. In addition, the Hundred Years' War raged between England and France. Confusion reigned, and the papacy was in no position to lead a widespread reforming movement. More and more people came to believe the ship of Peter was sinking. This was the context of Langland's great poem.

The situation was serious but not singular. For centuries—up to our own time—critics have blown loud trumpets warning of corruption in the Church. They have spun conspiracies and made charges that the Catholic Church has been infiltrated by everything from Aryans to Marxists, pagans to Freemasons, and family-interest groups to special-interest groups. This is nothing new: at times, wicked people have indeed undermined the Church, starting with Judas. The amazing thing is the Church has survived it all! Pointing zealously to such problems can help identify the enemy. Negatively, it can also feed the self-righteousness of the zealot and shift blame to vague figures far away. In this sense, the chant for reform can be unhealthy for our souls. The real question is perpetually, what are *we* going to do about reform in our own place and in our own time?

How did late medieval people think about and practice reform? What roadblocks held up the much-desired reformation of Christianity before the Protestants took matters into their own hands? Some kept up the call for reform while holding on to the principle of unity at the same time. Others started local grassroots movement of reform. Then there were the independent types who broke with the Church in the name of reform—even before Luther.

St. Catherine of Siena to the Pope: Be a Man!

One great example of late medieval reform was Catherine of Siena (1347–1380), a saint and Doctor of the Church. She knew the Church was the mystical body of Christ and the hope of the world. The popes represented Christ on earth. Therefore, Catherine was distressed by the fact that the popes resided in Avignon, France, and no longer in Rome, traditionally associated with Peter the apostle and his successors. As a lay member of the Dominican Order, she personally influenced Pope Gregory XI to return to Rome from Avignon in 1377. This was no easy task—for Catherine or Gregory. Insurrections and wars ravaged the Italian peninsula where the French pope was much hated. "Up, father, like a man!" Catherine composed in a letter to him, challenging him to put aside fear. Do not be timorous and do what you ought: return to Rome and use your authority to execute justice against the many iniquities in the Church, she challenged him. She believed reform from the top down would inspire the laity to reform their lives too.[2]

Gregory did return to Rome, but he unfortunately died in 1378. When the cardinals of the Church met to elect a new pope, Italian mobs broke into the voting chamber demanding an Italian be elected. The cardinals chose one, and he became Urban VI. In his fervor to begin reforms right away, Urban made enemies among the cardinals. Reformation was derailed, and the situation became much worse. The cardinals withdrew to try to annul his election and decide on an alternative French candidate who became Clement VII. Now there were two popes. The kingdoms of Europe lined up to support their favorite pope. This was reform gone bad.

Catherine was horrified. She composed a letter in 1378 to three Italian cardinals who defected from Urban. She demanded they support the true pope whom they had validly elected the first time—the one they accepted with everyone else and who received the office. By creating an antipope, "you have divided us from the truth which strengthens us," she warned. Pride robs you of the light of reason, and you have turned to the dark side, she charged. The pope represents Christ on earth, and you have broken obedience. Yield to the "prick of conscience that I know is perpetually stabbing you" for fostering disunity, she stated, and "feed in truth at the breast of the Bride of Christ."[3]

The schism lasted thirty-nine years. It had a devastating impact on widespread perceptions of the Church, its unity, and its authority. This happened at the very moment when rising national aspirations of the European peoples were straining against their common interests. At one point there were *three* claimants to the papacy! How could the situation possibly be resolved? At last, hundreds of churchmen and scholars met at the Council of Constance (1414–1418) to resolve the confusion. They deposed or accepted the resignation of all papal claimants and elected Pope Martin V (r. 1417–1431).

This was an important accomplishment. However, the Council of Constance also raised another problem: *conciliarism.* This is the theory that councils hold superior authority to popes. Conciliarism seemed to make sense due to the crisis of multiple claims to the papacy. Once the papacy stabilized again, conciliarism seemed a threat that made the popes of the late 1400s distrust councils altogether. Could new councils erode the authority of the papacy? Maybe it was better not to hold them. Tragically, this put off the question of systematic Church reform even further.

Grassroots Reform Movements

Without much papal leadership, by the late 1300s various laypeople, churchmen, and political rulers took reforming initiative into their own hands. The Brothers and Sisters of the Common Life, for example, were lay associations started in the Netherlands by the deacon Gerard Groote (1340–1384). They sought to develop a more vibrant inner life. Groote had been a well-off academic who passed through a conversion and spent time in a monastery. He emerged from this retreat with apostolic zeal, preaching widely. He was fearless in his attack on the vices of priests and monks. At one point he was forbidden by the bishop of his diocese to preach. Groote obeyed ecclesiastical authority and turned his attention to organizing communities of followers. This laid the basis for a fruitful reform movement.

Together, Groote and his followers focused on an inward piety known as *devotio moderna* ("modern devotion"). Intentional communities lived semi-monastic lives. They resolved to start a reform inside the Church, and their efforts were eventually approved by the pope. Through their schools and their writings—above all the *Imitation of Christ*, by Thomas à Kempis—the Brothers and Sisters of the Common Life influenced many beyond their immediate circle. That influence helped raise literacy rates (among women too) and book production in the Netherlands during the fifteenth and sixteenth centuries. This may have even unintentionally raised the level of economic prosperity there.

Up Close and Personal:
ST. CATHERINE OF GENOA

St. Catherine of Genoa is a stellar example of how God's grace can work through an individual who works steadily and faithfully, doing daily what seems small and relatively insignificant. Her deep and dedicated life of prayer prepared her heart to receive God's grace and sustained her in her difficult marriage and her work with the poor and neglected.

Born in 1447, Catherine married young to an irascible noble-man chosen by her family. He was unfaithful, was irresponsible with money, and had a violent temper. Catherine was miserable. She tried to find ways to cope by turning to worldly comforts until one day she experienced a profound conversion in prayer prior to the sacrament of Confession. God pierced her with his love, allowing her to experience its immense depth. She spent hours in prayer after this and became a daily communicant, yet always actuated her spiritual life in her daily duties. She cared for the sick in the hospital in Genoa for many years, eventually becoming an administrator there. She steadily endured the hor-rific plague the city faced in 1493, caring for those infected as nearly 80 percent of the city perished.

Eventually Catherine's prayer and steadfastness bore fruit in her personal life, and through God's grace her husband con-verted. He became a third order Franciscan, working alongside her in the hospital until his death. Afterward, she resigned from her duties because of her deteriorating health. She suffered greatly but took the time to speak to her spiritual director and a group of disciples about her life's experience. They set it down in writing.

God granted remarkable and mystical experiences to Cath-erine, particularly revelations about purgatory and the life of the soul. Her most widely known works, "Treatise on Purga-tory" and "Dialogue with a Soul," detail these. Later ratified by theologians, these works would go on to inspire many others, including other great saints of the Age of Reformations like St. Francis de Sales.

Her life and writings inspired her followers to form the Ora-tory of Divine Love, out of which came two significant church-men: Gian Pietro Carafa (1476–1559) and Gaetano da Thiene (1480–1547). They helped establish an order known as the The-atines that pursued innovative urban missionary work. This order later produced several reforming bishops.

Besides Groote, the Italian laywoman Catherine of Genoa (1447–1510) also left a great reforming legacy. Her life inspired a much later classic work in the philosophy of religion called *The Mystical Element of Religion as Studied in Saint Catherine of Genoa and Her Friends* (1908) by Friedrich von Hügel. Von Hügel thought of religion as made up of three elements: (1) religion as experiential, (2) religion as intellectual, and (3) religion as institutional (and thereby external, communal, and authoritative). Through his study of Catherine of Genoa and her friends, von Hügel concluded that one never finds any one of these three elements without a trace of the others. They properly go together for the fullest expression of religious life.

The difficulty in any religiously serious life was to *keep* these elements together. Enthused about one of them, believers all too easily suppress the others due to their longing to intensify (and thus simplify) their religion. For example, one who discovered the emotional/experiential side of religion would be tempted to "sweep aside both the external, as so much oppressive ballast; and the intellectual, as so much hair-splitting or rationalism." If those elements were swept aside, "a shifting subjectivity, and all but incurable tyranny of mood and fancy," would result, von Hügel predicted; "fanaticism is in full sight." On its own, mysticism tended toward subjectivism, intellectualism toward rationalism, and institutionalism toward superstition and routinization. In other words, in a healthy religious personality, each element needed to supplement, purify, and stimulate the other, protecting it from one-sided religion. The "cross" of religious existence meant the creative acceptance of the balance, tension, and friction of these elements *together*.[4] True reform maintained harmony among religious experience, reason, and institution, as von Hügel found in Catherine of Genoa and her friends. This required spiritual docility and patience.

Sacrificing Unity for the Sake of Reform: John Wycliffe and Jan Hus

Other late medieval reformers did not manage to balance these three elements. They ended up creating heretical movements. For example, there was the religious reform movement started by the Oxford professor and priest John Wycliffe (1330–1384) whose members were popularly denounced as "Lollards," though it is not clear what that term meant. Wycliffe condemned the widespread Church corruption of his day. He also appealed to the Bible as the highest authority and pushed reading it in the vernacular or common language. On that basis, he criticized the rule of clerical celibacy, monasticism, intercession of the saints, veneration of images and relics, pilgrimages, transubstantiation, and papal authority. He also thought the property of unworthy officials and clerics should be taken away.

Wycliffe attracted a wide following across England. From the perspective of von Hügel's elements of religion, Wycliffe emphasized the intellectual element in religion (he was a professor) at the expense of the institutional side. This sacrificed the unity of the Church and ended in heresy.

In addition, Wycliffe's teaching inspired another academic and priest, Jan Hus (ca. 1372–1415), a Czech thinker in Eastern Europe. Hus vigorously attacked Church corruption. That was nothing new, as many had done the same. However, Hus went a step further to insist that sinful clergy could have no real authority—a heresy like that of the Donatists dealt with by St. Augustine in the 400s. Such clergy should be removed from office and their property confiscated. That appealed to a wide spectrum of people in a region where the churchmen owned nearly half of the land. Hus gained followers. He appealed to scripture, history, and conscience against the authority of the papacy. Because the papacy was still divided by two—and then three—claimants, this lent weight to Hus's arguments. "To rebel against an erring pope is to obey Christ the Lord," he wrote in his *Treatise on the Church*.[5] As with Wycliffe, zeal against corruption supported the belief that the Church was irredeemable. As a result, Wycliffe's and Hus's efforts threatened the unity of the Church.

Hus was eventually burned as a heretic, sparking anger and revolt. One branch of his followers, called the Taborites, became militant radicals with an apocalyptic desire to bring about the kingdom of God on earth by force. There would be no private property—everything would be held in common. This revolutionary movement inaugurated two decades of violence in the Hussite Wars before Taborite forces fell in defeat. Reforming radicalism, which called for overturning the social order, would reemerge in the sixteenth century with bloody results in Germany.

Reform by Catholic Monarchs

Elsewhere, political leaders took the initiative in Church reform. This occurred in Spain under the governance of King Ferdinand II and Queen Isabella. These two Catholic monarchs famously supported Christopher Columbus on his voyage across the Atlantic Ocean in 1492. They also launched Spain's Golden Age during the 1500s. After centuries of anarchic fighting between regional lords around Spain, the monarchs devoted themselves to shaping a new national identity through unity in the Catholic faith. Their devotion to the faith and their awareness of corruption in the Church prompted their great concern for reform. Along with their advisors they strove to raise the standards for the episcopacy, the priests, and the religious orders through discipline and education. These efforts met determined resistance in places—as when hundreds of friars fled to North Africa and converted to Islam rather than give up their female companions.

One important Spanish reformer in league with Ferdinand and Isabella was the cardinal and statesman Francisco Jiménez de Cisneros (1436–1517). He served as Isabella's spiritual director for a time. When she secured the archbishopric of Toledo for him, he tried to refuse the honor. Ordered by Rome to take it up, however, Cisneros obeyed but continued to live simply. He dedicated himself to reforming his region of Spain *in capite et in membris* (in head and in members). Cisneros mandated that clerics live in their parishes, placed harsh penalties on clerics who broke their vows of celibacy or lived with common-law wives, and required clerics to preach every Sunday and to go to Confession regularly. To influence the wider lay population, he pushed the translation and publication of devotional texts. Thanks to the new printing press, this flooded bookstalls with works strengthening faith and holiness, a large number of which were in the vernacular rather than Latin for widespread appeal. One of these books would end up in the hands of Ignatius of Loyola, changing his life and the later course of Catholic reform.

YOU BE THE JUDGE:

Didn't the Inquisition kill and torture people because of their faith?

The Spanish Inquisition has a terrible reputation. In fact, it is the stuff of legends. Recently, twentieth-century scholars have gained access to meticulously kept court records and have begun to show just how much is myth and how much really happened. Surprisingly, though the court perpetrated abuses at certain times, it was quite progressive compared to other courts of its time.

There were various inquisitional courts set up in different countries from the thirteenth to the nineteenth centuries. Different regions dealt with different problems or heresies. These courts had judges, or inquisitors, who examined cases of professed Christian persons accused of heterodoxy. Various saints whose activities looked suspicious at first faced inquisitions in their region, including St. Ignatius of Loyola (St. Teresa of Ávila was accused but never tried).

The most famous was the Spanish Inquisition, which began in 1478 under the rule of King Ferdinand and Queen Isabella. Pope Sixtus IV soon regretted allowing the Spanish monarchy to govern this inquisition because the church could not easily step in to alleviate its severity or mitigate the politics involved.

The political context for the Spanish Inquisition makes its problems evident. In an effort to unify and stabilize their country, the monarchs had expelled the Jewish population from Spain and also broken the Treaty of Granada by making it effectively illegal to be Muslim. At the time, the Muslims were viewed as a threat because they had just conquered Christian Constantinople in 1453 and pushed deep into south-east Europe. Also, because of the close link between Church and state at the time, rulers were more likely to consider other faiths as a threat to the faith of their own people. The Jewish and Muslim population who had converted were most often targeted as potential threats. The perception of heresy in terms of race and cultural differences created a strong bias that led to expulsions. The pope had allowed the court to be controlled by the monarchy because he was hoping it would quell the religious fervor that had gripped the country in the name of national unity—and the riots, denunciations, and pogroms that were rampant. Unfortunately, the monarchy trespassed on the rights and religious freedom of entire populations in their efforts to preserve unity and used the inquisitional courts to enforce this. It was during these first few decades that the most people were executed, possibly up to two thousand.[6] When Cardinal Cisneros became grand inquisitor in 1506, he reformed the system to get rid of abuses.

Interestingly, many advances the inquisition made are still used in law systems today. Things like using a grand jury to determine if a case is worth trying, the need for multiple witnesses, and various ways in which defendants could protect themselves throughout the legal process endured.

Legends say thousands or even millions of people were executed in the Spanish Inquisition. New scholarship has found it was fewer than most people believed. It was probably closer to three to five thousand people over the 350 years of operation, with the first several decades being the worst. Scholarship has shown the court was also more lenient than civil courts of the time, in both its use of torture and the number of executions. There are even stories that people who had been accused of civil crimes would commit a religious one so they would be tried in the inquisition instead—they had a chance at being treated better, more fairly, and were more likely to make it out alive.[7]

This does nothing to excuse the reality that people were killed because of their faith. But the communities of the time truly saw heterodoxy as a threat to the souls of others in the community. They believed it was necessary to take measures to protect their communities from others who would lead them astray and cause social upheaval. Religious wars and rebellions were not uncommon at the time—what would happen in the Münster Rebellion is precisely what the Spanish monarchy was hoping to avoid in their own country.

The context of the time makes the Inquisition more understandable, but it does not fully justify it or its methods, especially when considered against modern-day understandings of religious freedom. The Spanish monarchs truly desired to keep their country safe from religious violence but did so by perpetrating a smaller-scale and more controlled version of religious violence! Though the Spanish Inquisition did not slaughter millions as rumored, it was still a tool used dominate.

Cisneros's greatest achievement was to establish the University of Alcalá in 1508 to forward reform through a better educated clergy. The goal was to promote both medieval and Renaissance modes of learning. This university attracted the best and the brightest and became a center of reforming fervor. Men trained there—such as Diego Laynez, the second superior general of the Jesuits—would play leading roles at the Council of Trent when it began in 1543.

In these ways, the initiative of Ferdinand, Isabella, Cisneros, and many other Spanish Catholics thoroughly reformed the Church in Spain. The country became a formidable bastion of the faith, strongly resistant to the spread of Protestant ideas when they emerged. The powerful forces of state formation like in Spain would shape the ways later Protestant reformations unfolded.

State Formation

In contrast to fragmented political units of the Middle Ages, the emergence of national sentiment aided the gradual formation of modern states just before and during the Age of Reformations (like what happened in Spain). *States* were defined by territorial boundaries and their power secured by war, trade, and sophisticated administration. State formation marked the beginning of the modern age, and it affected the Papal States in central Italy too. The Papal States provided temporal power, protection, and financial stability to the papacy based in Rome. It was a priority of the popes to secure their temporal power in the Papal States between 1417 when the Council of Constance resolved the Great Western Schism and the beginning of Luther's reformation in 1517.

That papal effort of state formation drew the Renaissance popes (1417–1521) deeply into temporal concerns. They produced many glorious fruits, such as the inauguration of the new St. Peter's Basilica as the greatest church structure in the world, and some of the finest art in existence, such as the Sistine Chapel. However, none of the Renaissance popes are now recognized as saints or even as "blesseds" or "venerables." There are significant reasons for that. Three of these popes in particular illustrate how worldly temptations tragically delayed systematic reform on the very eve of the Protestant Reformations.

Roadblocks to Reform: Temptations to Flesh, Politics, and Art

Pope Alexander VI (r. 1492–1503) gave in to severe temptations of the flesh. His main mistress before his papal election was the Roman beauty Vannozza Cattanei, and with her he had four children. As a cardinal, he amassed a fortune. It enabled him to make gifts to other cardinals and smooth his path to the papacy. As the historian Henri Daniel-Rops wrote, Alexander VI was one of those thorough-going sensualists who arrange everything to suit his own pleasure.[8] He pursued affairs with several women and fathered more children even as pope. The scandal was magnified by the fact that he paraded his children in the open and lavished gifts on them, including Church offices.

It was no wonder the popular Dominican preacher Girolamo Savon-arola (1452–1498) attacked Rome and its vices as a new Babylon from his pulpit in Florence. It is in these two figures—Alexander VI and Savona-rola—one sees the total breakdown in the relationship between the principle of reform and the principle of authority. Savonarola was an extraordinarily popular and controversial figure. He possessed an incredible talent for persuasive oration. Everyone stood transfixed in his vast audiences. He believed it was his mission to proclaim the ruinous state of the Church.

Savonarola said the bride of Christ was tainted with sin and must be purified. He was determined to shed light on abuses and demanded reform. Was the corrupt Alexander VI still the rightful head of the Church? God should punish him! "It is by the gates that the house is entered," Savonarola said in a sermon of 1493. It is the clergy "who should lead the faithful into the Church of Christ." Churchmen have not only destroyed the Church of God but also "built up another after their own fashion." They have formed a new church—not of living Christians but of dry sticks.[9] Protestant reformers would soon make similar claims.

Meanwhile, Savonarola began to mix religion and politics to get laws passed against sin in Florence. In fact, he slowly imposed a theocratic dictatorship on the city. Faith became an integralist ideology. People began to renounce worldly pleasures with panicked fervor. Women gave up their jewels and fine clothes. Men quit going to brothels. Bankers returned money wrongly acquired. Bands of young men roamed the city terrorizing public sinners.

Convinced of his divine mission, Savonarola defied the pope's order to cease preaching. But his authority began to erode, and the pope pushed the city to punish him. He and two companions were burnt at the stake.

Savonarola's legacy remained controversial. He rightly called for reform, but he made many mistakes. He was too noisy and political. St. Catherine of Siena had also criticized popes and clergy, but she thought it the highest Christian duty to remain loyal to the office of the papacy as the center of unity—no matter what. She believed one must never give up on the hope for reform through the power of the Holy Spirit in the life of an individual. A later saint like Philip Neri (1515–1595) admired Savonarola's passion for reform, but Neri was quiet and obedient to the Church. He succeeded in reform where Savonarola failed. The personal weaknesses of "authority" and the personal excesses of "reform" in the 1490s set the stage for the Protestant Reformations twenty years later.

Up Close and Personal:
ST. PHILIP NERI

St. Philip Neri spent much of his life evangelizing the laity of Rome, earning the title "Apostle of Rome." He inspired reform by encouraging communion between persons who loved, learned, and worshipped together in the Congregation of the Oratory he founded in 1575. This group of priests and laymen took no formal vows (it was not a religious order) yet were bound together in charity. Oratories like these spread throughout the world and are still active today. In fact, they are often mentioned in the accounts of other saints and influential Catholic thinkers, such as St. John Henry Newman.

Philip was born in Florence in 1515. Rejecting the business world of his family, he went to Rome to study philosophy and theology at the Sapienza and Sant'Agostino while working as a tutor for two young boys. He visited the poor and sick, using his good cheer to comfort and elevate them. He spent many hours in prayer and visited the seven pilgrim churches of Rome on a regular basis (he would take groups of people on pilgrimage to these sites). He lived a very simple life as a layman, befriending many people, including great men like St. Ignatius of Loyola, St. Charles Borromeo, and St. Francis de Sales.

In 1548, he founded the Confraternity of the Most Holy Trinity to care for the pilgrims who were poor, sick, or still recovering from illnesses. Much like the Oratory would do, this confraternity also met for prayer, for devotions, and to listen to Philip's preaching. Eventually acquiring a church and a nearby house, the fraternity set up a hospital-hospice that served many.

After many years as a layman pursuing holiness, a spiritual director encouraged him to take orders. His ordination in 1551 did not fundamentally alter his approach to communion with and evangelization of the laity in Rome, nor did it alter his jolly demeanor. He was known to play practical jokes, poke fun at himself, and use humor to seek humility. He continued to endear himself to many while changing their hearts and helping them become closer to God.

Philip had to endure papal suspicion because of the success and reforming character of the movements he founded. His success in attracting disciples and in evangelizing caused jealousies and inspired rumors of dissension or even rebellion that reached Paul IV in 1559. Philip's work was suspended for a brief time. Happily, his successor, Pius IV, dismissed such rumors and Philip was free to continue his ministries. Other rumors would surface surrounding the Oratory less than a decade later, requiring an intervention from Cardinal Charles Borromeo to save the group until it received approbation from Gregory XIII.

Philip had many mystical experiences, such as levitations during prayer, but the most dramatic happened at the catacomb of San Sebastiano. There he experienced a physical enlargement of his heart, filled with profound love, that stayed with him for the rest of his life.

Temptations of Politics

The lady of Langland's vision at the beginning of this chapter was beautiful because she represented "Holy Church" in its ultimate heavenly glory. If one viewed the Church as merely a worldly institution concerned with money and power, its beauty would no longer appear as clearly. Without acknowledging its transcendent dimension, the Church looked like any other earthly institution, dirtied by the filth of temporal conflict. This was the problem with Pope Julius II's papacy (r. 1503–1513).

Julius had a violent temper and was known as the "warrior pope" for his military campaigns to restore the temporal authority of the papacy. He chose his name in emulation of Julius Caesar (much like Pope Alexander VI had chosen his in emulation of Alexander the Great). Sometimes he personally led troops into battle. He dreamed of a united Italy under the leadership of Rome as the spiritual and cultural capital. His political actions were often "Machiavellian" and seemed devoid of ethics. In fact, the Italian diplomat Niccolò Machiavelli (1469–1527) took inspiration from Julius in his famous book *The Prince*, written during the years of Julius's pontificate. Machiavelli admired Julius's hardy impetuosity in securing his political goals and in forcing other rulers to tremble before the power of the Church. Julius's actions compromised the spiritual authority of his office and eventually contributed to a crisis of conscience within the German monk Martin Luther. Luther visited Rome in 1510 during Julius's papacy and was scandalized by what he saw and heard.

Temptations of Art

The third temptation for the Renaissance-era papacy was art. Julius II commissioned the painting of the Sistine Chapel by Michelangelo and inaugurated the building of St. Peter's Basilica. These were truly great achievements. However, the next pope, Leo X (r. 1513–1521), seemed to let his passion for art be his reason for living. As Daniel-Rops wrote, his pontificate showed how "when the cult of intelligence and beauty loses its sense of proportion and makes intellectual and artistic creations an end in themselves, it too constitutes a formidable spiritual temptation."[10]

Leo X was elected during the Fifth Lateran Council (1512–1517), but he seemed to have no interest in implementing its proposed reforms. His main concern was the cultured life of the intellect and the arts. It seemed his most important duty was the acquisition of books and the protection of scholars and artists. They flocked to the papal court, and he handed out money. St. Peter's slowly rose from the ground, exciting him greatly. Leo granted new indulgences in return for financial contributions. Indulgence preachers made their way into Germany as sparks into a tinderbox.

The Renaissance

The flowering of art—and its temptations—linked the Renaissance to the Age of Reformations. The word "Renaissance" means "rebirth." It emerged out of the rebirth of classical learning and art in Europe in the

1300s. The migration of Greek scholars from the Byzantine Empire that had been conquered in 1453 by the Ottomans increased the knowledge of Greek language and texts. This gave rise to *humanism* in education and scholarship. Humanism was shaped by the interests of educated laypeople in poetry, history, and moral philosophy and contrasted with medieval scholasticism's focus on clerical learning in theology and logic. Humanist scholars applied their new linguistic skills to biblical studies, and they worked to integrate this new learning with Christianity.

In addition, Renaissance builders and artists recovered classical ideals of beauty. People wondered at the noble dignity and awesome natural powers of human beings created by God. They had confidence they could achieve great things—as in the bold plans of Pope Julius II to build the grandest building in Christendom, St. Peter's. Renaissance self-assurance propelled Michelangelo to paint the Sistine Chapel and Leonardo da Vinci to dream of flying machines.

Inspired by these possibilities, the great humanist scholar Desiderius Erasmus (1466–1536) hoped in 1517 for "the near approach of a golden age." Three of the chief blessings of humanity were about the be restored, he predicted: true Christian piety, which had fallen into decay; learning of the best sort (humanism); and "the public and lasting [peace] of Christendom."[11] He was overconfident. Soon after, Erasmus was bemoaning the divided state of Christian Europe as different reformers and their followers combatted each other, sometimes violently.

Humanism and Its Reform Ideal

During his lifetime, Erasmus witnessed the passing of the medieval world and the emergence of a new age. This new age possessed a new slogan to guide reform: *ad fontes*—"return to the sources!" This was the highest ideal of Renaissance humanists: go back to the original texts of the classical and early Christian worlds. They believed *ad fontes* would bring true cultural and religious reform. Historian Carlos M. N. Eire wrote, "Ancient languages, ancient wisdom, ancient arts, ancient piety—all became undisputed models to follow, blueprints for a brighter future."[12]

This idealization of the distant past inculcated a new view of history: the time between the ancient golden age and the rebirth of light in the present time was a "middle age." Many thought this middle age lacked humanist sophistication and pure religion, so it was also a *dark age*. Seeing the millennium from around AD 400 to 1400 as a distinct period was a powerful insight from the Renaissance. It marked, quite literally, the beginning of modern history as a distinct concept.

This new view of history profoundly influenced the ideal of reform. Nostalgia for the classical age cast a shadow over one thousand years of the Christian past. The people in the "middle age" between ancient and modern did not "really" know the Gospel. Corruptions had leaked in and obscured the classical purity of Christ. Christianity was mired in scholasticism. The idea became widespread in the 1500s that true reform required one to skip over those centuries in the quest for the original truth. This downgraded the sense of continuity and tradition represented by the Church.

Renaissance humanism paved the way for the Protestant Reformations, but it did not cause them. For example, Erasmus never left the Catholic Church. The humanist Thomas More died for his Catholic faith. But the humanist view of history made it possible to redefine the medieval world as irrelevant and justify new ideas of reform for a new age.

The Donation of Constantine

A damaging Renaissance discovery seemed to confirm the view that the Middle Ages were dark and corrupt. It was made by the humanist scholar and priest Lorenzo Valla (ca. 1407–1457). In 1440, he worked as court secretary and historian for Alfonso V of Aragon, who was involved in a territorial dispute with the papacy. Valla analyzed one of the texts most often used by the papacy to defend its rulership of central Italy, the Donation of Constantine. This document supposedly dated from the fourth century. It was used to prove Constantine had given wide secular authority to the popes over Italy and beyond, and that the pope of Rome possessed authority over all bishops in the world. Valla doubted its authenticity. By studying the Latin of the document and contrasting it with the Latin of known fourth-century texts, he determined it was forged. The Donation of Constantine was full of words and concepts, such as "fief," that did not even exist yet in the fourth century. Valla wrote that this fake document was "not the utterance of Constantine, but of some fool of a priest."[13] Scholars today believe the document dates to the late eighth century.

It is important to note that the spiritual authority of the papacy does not rely on the approval of any secular power, Constantine or otherwise. In the teaching and tradition of the Church, it is based on Jesus's words to Peter in the scriptures and early Church practice (tradition). Nevertheless, in the confusing mix of church and state during the time, Valla's discovery was a blow to the public image of the Church as a religious authority.

Up Close and Personal:

THE PAPACY IN SCRIPTURE AND THE CHURCH FATHERS

There are lots of examples of Peter's primacy among the apostles in the gospels. A key passage is in Matthew 16:16–19, when Peter professes Jesus as the Messiah. Jesus renames him "Cephas," the rock on which he builds his Church. He also gives the power to bind and loose. Peter is again set apart in Luke 22:31–32, when Jesus prays for his faith specifically and commands him to strengthen his brethren.

Peter is mentioned 191 times in the New Testament. The next most frequently mentioned apostle is John at 48 times. Peter is most often listed first (see Matthew 10:2; Mark 3:16; Luke 6:14; Acts 1:13, etc.); most often speaks for the apostles (see Matthew 18:21; Mark 8:29; Luke 9:5, 12:41; John 6:67, etc.); and is most often the leader of the apostles (see Mark 16:7; Acts 1:22; Acts 2:37–41, 5:15; Acts 4:1–13; Acts 15:7–11, etc.). There is strong scriptural evidence identifying Peter as the head of the Church and the first pope, and many of the early Church Fathers agreed on this as well.

Writing in AD 251, St. Cyprian of Carthage reflected, "Indeed, the others [Apostles] were that also which Peter was; but a primacy is given to Peter, whereby it is made clear that there is but one Church and one chair. . . . If someone does not hold fast to this unity of Peter, can he imagine that he still holds the faith? If he [should] desert the chair of Peter upon whom the Church was built, can he still be confident that he is in the Church?"[14]

St. Irenaeus writes in AD 189, "For with this Church [Rome], because of its superior origin, all Churches must agree, that is, all the faithful in the whole world; and it is in her that the faithful everywhere have maintained the Apostolic tradition."[15]

Pope St. Damasus I asserts:

> The holy Roman Church has been placed at the forefront not by the conciliar decisions of other churches, but has received the primacy by the evangelic voice of our Lord and Savior, who says: "You are Peter, and upon this rock I will build my Church, and the gates of hell will not prevail against it; and I will give to you the keys of the kingdom of heaven . . . ."
>
> . . . The first see, therefore, is that of Peter the Apostle, that of the Roman Church, which has neither stain nor blemish nor anything like it.[16]

Valla had used textual criticism and historical logic to prove the papal document was a medieval invention. Humanists scholars who knew the past had to agree with him. This seemed to reveal a whole new layer of corruption. Historian Eire wrote, "The church was corrupt not just because of abuses and clerical misbehavior, but also because it had twisted the truth itself."[17] Valla's *Falsely Believed and Forged Donation of Constantine* was printed in Germany in 1517, just as Martin Luther came on the scene.

The Printing Press and Reform

There was one more important factor affecting late medieval reform and Renaissance humanism to consider: the printing press. The goldsmith, inventor, and publisher Johannes Gutenberg (ca. 1400–1468) first started printing documents with mechanical moveable type around 1439. Within sixty years, the consumer demands of Catholic religious culture propelled the business success of printing. Missals, psalters, breviaries, books of hours, grammars, primers, and indulgences flowed from the presses. The structure of books quickly matured into the form known today, with title pages, dedications, indexes, and side notes.

Eventually, a wild profusion of books altered the worlds of both knowledge and faith. Major centers of print developed in Augsburg, Nuremberg, and Basel—all cities that would take up new Protestant messages of reform with enthusiasm. From these cities, the international book market spread the new ideas of reform far and wide at a reasonable price. Trading caravans transported books hundreds of miles to huge book fairs, like the one in Frankfurt, Germany. These developments not only made the Reformations possible because of wide communication but also laid the basis for the later Age of Enlightenment and knowledge-based economies of modern times.

After Luther emerged as one of the first celebrity authors, controversy over rival ideas of reform transformed the German printing industry. Six to seven million Protestant pamphlets appeared on the market during the first volatile decade after Luther started writing. Publishers made huge sums, though some refused to publish the new ideas.

All of this gave the impression that a new age had indeed dawned. Protestants even hoped the printing press might mean the end of the papacy. The Protestant historian John Foxe (1516–1587) published his famous *Actes and Monuments* in 1563. This book told the stories of Protestants martyred at the hands of the Catholic Queen Mary of England. It also credited the printing press as an organ of the Holy Spirit to reveal how the pope was Antichrist to more and more people. "God hath opened the Press to preach," Foxe wrote. "I suppose, that either the pope must abolish printing, or . . . printing doubtless will abolish him." Lack of knowledge and ignorance made the pope strong in the past, Foxe thought; "Nothing doth debilitate and shake the high spire of [the] papacy so much, as reading, preaching, knowledge, and judgment."[18]

Foxe exaggerated. Catholics such as Cisneros in Spain had already made good use of printing technology. In addition, not far from papal Rome, the first printing press in Italy was established by German monks at the Benedictine Abbey of Saint Scholastica in 1465. In fact, one of the oldest surviving printed documents in existence is an indulgence issued by Pope Nicholas V in 1454. Printing presses served the papacy too. In England, printing presses churned out Catholic works by the thousands in the decades before Foxe: liturgical books, letters of indulgence for hospitals and other charities, a vast range of devotional tracts to promote Catholic faith and practice, pamphlets on the merits of the rosary, lives of the saints, and sermons. Lay demand for vernacular religious books among Catholics *preceded* the Protestant Reformations.

Nevertheless, printing represented a new factor in the religious controversy, and Catholics struggled to keep up. There was a need to dramatically readjust expectations and catechetical methods for a growing literate culture.

Oral and Literate Cultures Created Challenges for Reform

The ongoing transition from oral to literate culture at this time was even more significant in history than the one from print to digital media in the twenty-first century. Without a doubt, printing changed the world, including the world of religion. It was the coming of a new culture of text. Historian Eamon Duffy wrote that "behind the repudiation of ceremonial by the [Protestant] reformers lay a radically different conceptual world, a world in which text was everything, sign [or sacrament] nothing."[19] This quotation neatly encapsulates the contrast between oral and literate cultures.

In the Middle Ages before the printing press and wide availability of books of any kind, the literate and the illiterate both expressed their faith through common rituals like the Mass. These rituals maintained the people's relationship to God and to each other. For most people, religious life centered not on theology or mysticism or the Bible as a stand-alone text but on a cycle of ceremonies and practices performed in their locale meant to communicate scriptural truths. Beyond the liturgy, these practices involved shrines, images, religious plays, prayers for miracles, festivals, pilgrimage sites, relics, and works of charity often performed with others though confraternities (much like "church societies" today). Many theologians worried that common people did not distinguish enough between the saints in heaven and the images of them on earth. Moralists mocked the relic vendors trying to hawk feathers of St. Michael the archangel's wing or the hay beneath the crib at Bethlehem. Nevertheless, laity continued to lovingly adorn their statues and their relics and to venerate them. They believed in the objective power of holy words, gestures, and things as signs of spiritual power to win favor and to ward away evil.

People related to the world of faith through their bodies. Material things supported their desire to attain spiritual realities. *Thought* was not enough. Faith was joined to works as naturally as external ritual was joined to internal prayer. "James the gentle has judged in his letters that faith without works is vain and idle," the beautiful woman representing Holy Church told William Langland in his poem, paraphrasing James 2:26.[20] In addition, rituals were needed to establish set procedures that allowed people to perform meaningful actions together in order to align themselves with the divine. In a way, St. Catherine of Siena, an illiterate woman who nevertheless became a Doctor of the Church, exemplified the heights of this old oral-culture Christianity. She recorded that Jesus and St. Thomas Aquinas appeared to her later in life and taught her to read, so she really represented a bridge between the two cultures.

In the generations after the printing press, the importance of certain rituals and the physical in the earlier oral culture started to give way to a new form of culture. Literacy and a love of texts encouraged a modern consciousness with greater abstraction and intellectualism that was more widespread across the population. Literacy increased. Disembodied texts easily isolated writers and readers from each other. This shifted the focus of Christians from listening to reading, aligning spiritual authority more with texts than with people. Knowledge was gained from individual engagement with those texts, not so much from the community and from elders who had received oral testimony from their ancestors. "By storing knowledge outside the mind," one historian wrote, print downgraded "the figures of the wise old man and the wise old woman, repeaters of the past, in favor of younger discoverers of something new."[21] It is interesting to note none of the major Protestant reformers were over the age of thirty-seven when their movements began. They were all born in the 1480s and 1490s, forty to fifty years after the Gutenberg printing press. Most of them were ex-Catholic priests, theologically educated through texts. Someone like Erasmus, who was born in 1466, retained a stronger connection to the older oral culture and stayed with the Church even while being a strong critic.

Literate culture was not necessarily "better" than oral culture or vice versa. In fact, there is a dynamic tension between orality and literacy in Christian culture that changes due to historical context. As the "Word" of God, Jesus Christ is spoken by God the Father, not written by him. Jesus himself did not leave any writings behind. "I am the way, the truth, and the life," he said. The apostles knew him through sound, sight, and touch. Yet at the same time, the "word" of God or the written scriptures is a foundation of Christianity.[22] Both orality and literacy nourish Christian culture.

Widespread attention to the text of the scriptures due to Renaissance humanism and the printing press led some to think of God's revelation differently. Some started to think God had revealed himself most importantly through the *written* word, or scripture, and not as much through the incarnation, the Eucharist, or tradition handed on from the apostles. Even Catholic scholars such as Erasmus pursued this line of thought. "Biblicism" emerged among some reformers who wanted whole societies, not just churches, to model themselves on literal biblical precedent.

In addition, the new literate culture emphasized how the spiritual is superior to the physical, and the internal to the external. This sort of spiritualism came in part from reaction against worldly clerics and abuses of things like relics and indulgences, but also from the individualized nature of engaging the written word. And it came from the Renaissance. Along with the revival of ancient pagan thought, particularly of Plato, there came a "metaphysics of suspicion" toward the material world, Eire wrote.[23] This mentality inevitably downgraded the institutional (external) elements of religion in favor of the intellectual and mystical elements, throwing the traditional idea of reform off balance, from the Catholic point of view.

When Cardinal Reginald Pole (1500–1558) helped to restore the Catholic faith in England after Queen Mary came to the throne in 1553, he understood the difference between the two cultures. Pole had a deep sense of the value of reading and preaching scripture. But he "abhorred religious argument and the spirit of self-sufficiency which he believed indiscriminate Bible-reading by lay people was likely to encourage," the historian Eamon Duffy wrote. Pole thought it was better for people to absorb the faith through participating body and soul in the liturgy and sacraments of the Church. He wrote that people want to fast-track to God through the reading of books. But isolated reading could easily lead to heresy. He concluded that those who were obedient, who sought faith in the community of ceremonies, were more likely to receive light than those who mainly read books and risked misunderstanding.[24]

Oral and literate cultures continued to exist side by side at the start of the Age of Reformations. They were forces molding and twisting the idea of reform until the tension became unbearable, in some cases breaking the bond between the principle of reform and the principle of Church authority or unity. Political instability, worldly temptations, the formation of national sentiment and states, humanism, and the printing press created revolutionary conditions during the Age of Reformations.

Chapter 2

Protestants

Who Was Martin Luther?

Martin Luther (1483–1546) was a pivotal figure in the history of reform. He was born in central Germany to an ambitious, hardworking, and strict middle-class family. His father pushed him toward a career in law. In preparation, Luther pursued a liberal arts education. He immersed himself in the new textual culture that made the ancient classics, Church Fathers, and medieval thinkers widely available. Luther's father invested heavily in this education, and his son performed well. Luther graduated with a master of arts degree in 1505. His father purchased the legal textbooks his son would need to continue his studies, and even had a wealthy bride in mind for him.

A chance thunderstorm changed his life and the course of history. It happened while traveling back to his university to continue his legal studies. A bolt of lightning struck near him, and he was thrown to the ground by the air pressure. In a panic, he cried out: "Help, St. Anne, I will become a monk!"[1] He survived and continued on his journey, resolved to take his rash oath seriously.

This event reveals much about Luther and his times. St. Anne was the patroness of miners. Luther's father was in the mining business, so she was likely invoked in the household as Luther matured. Medieval Catholicism emphasized the place of mediation in the relationship between God and human beings. Ideally, saints, sacraments and sacramentals, and the Church bridged individual religious lives, linking them to each other and to God. Sometimes this mediation could become idolatrous or superstitious. Luther struck a bargain: you do this for me, and I will do this for you. If St. Anne would rescue him, he would become a monk. This tragically bypassed the deeper question of God's will in his vocation.

Luther may have chosen the Augustinians because of their strict asceticism, academic bent, and devotion to St. Anne. They were the "progressive" order of the day, pursuing reform within themselves and reaching out to the wider society through their mobile and popular preachers. The Augustinians were focused on personal study of the scriptures, and this seems to have been highly attractive to Luther. The Augustinian friars would be Luther's earliest supporters as he became known as a reformer himself. Evangelical reform in both its Catholic and Lutheran varieties would spread widely through the Augustinian preachers during the 1520s.

Sola Fide

Luther was ordained a priest in 1507. In 1510, he traveled to Rome as a representative for an internal Augustinian dispute over how best to reform the order. Pope Julius II and his court were away at the time. However, small-town Luther was shocked by the opulence of the "big city." Indignant, he eventually lost faith in the Holy Spirit's working through the institutional Church.

Internally, Luther suffered from scrupulosity and spiritual despair. He had acquired a certain pessimism about the role of human reason and will in relation to God from his education. He doubted the purity of his own intentions in his attempts to diligently practice monastic life. He spent hours in Confession. How could he know if he was doing things enough or correctly? He was angry with God and did not love him.

Johann von Staupitz (ca. 1460–1524) was Luther's learned and kind spiritual adviser. Staupitz was a leading figure in the Bible-based reform movement emerging among the Augustinians. He was devoted to biblical scholarship, pastoral ministry, and Christo-centric spirituality. He helped Luther overcome his religious fear. Luther was always grateful to him for giving "birth to me in Christ."[2] Staupitz knew Luther needed to have more to do than stew in self-scrutiny. So he sent him to Wittenberg in eastern Germany to study theology. There Luther adopted the method of the Renaissance: return *ad fontes*, to the original sources, accessed through ancient languages. He also taught students and pastored at a nearby village parish.

In his academic study of scripture brought on by monastic obedience, Luther began to find answers to his deep questions. He became one of the best-known interpreters of the Bible in all Christian history. Working with the psalms, Luther thought he made a breakthrough: "My God, my God, why have you forsaken me?" (Ps 22:1). Had God also experienced inner despair in Jesus as Luther had felt for so long? It seemed so. Jesus had taken upon himself sin and the alienation that flowed from it. Luther discovered a new and deeper trust in God, and a more defined question: how exactly is one saved?

As he tried to answer this question, he wrestled with Romans 1:17, a verse that had long terrified him: "He through faith is righteous shall live." The details of Luther's inner development at this point are not clear. It seems one day in the library tower of his cloister in Wittenberg, Luther experienced an insight into this passage that led him to a sense of peace. A merciful God justifies by faith—not works. God treats one as righteous on account of the work of Christ. One's own works do not have to be enough. "This made me feel as if I had been born again and passed through open doors into paradise itself," he wrote. "All of Scripture appeared different to me now."[3] This "tower experience" slowly convinced Luther all theology should rest on the scriptures. He came to believe the key to the entire Bible was Paul's writings on faith. His *sola fide* or "faith alone" theology was slowly emerging.

This theology would be the basis from which he judged bishops, councils, and popes. "He who does not accept my doctrine cannot be saved,"

Luther wrote; "for it is God's and not mine." In 1520, Luther stated that in matters of faith, "each Christian is for himself Pope and Church, and nothing may be decreed or kept that could issue in a threat to faith." This created a clash between his allegiance to the Church and his own theological opinions. He came to believe if he abandoned *sola fide*, it would amount to apostasy against himself.[4]

The *Ninety-Five Theses* (1517)

Luther's German context matters a great deal for understanding what happened next. Germans had long complained about papal authority and financial policies that seemed to encourage abuses and extortion of German money. For example, Pope Leo X granted an indulgence to draw money to Rome for the building of St. Peter's Basilica. Behind the scenes, this money also helped Archbishop Albrecht of Mainz (1490–1545) pay off the debt he incurred when he purchased his see of high political influence.

The theology behind indulgences rests on the understanding that sin by its nature entails a double consequence. Grave sin leads to eternal separation from God or eternal punishment in hell. The second consequence of sin is that it produces unhealthy attachment to creatures and created goods that need to be purified during life on earth or after death in purgatory (called "temporal punishment"). This punishment is not lasting but is needed in order to detach the soul from the things of the world. Indulgences were granted not for the forgiveness of sins but for the reduction of this temporal punishment resulting from sin. They were exercises to deepen attachment to God and to reduce the second consequence of sin. They involved prayer, acts of charity, or penance as a way of cooperating in the graces of Christ's redemption to purify the Christian's soul.

Distributing indulgences in exchange for alms was an established practice at the time. Those alms could then be used by the Church for various purposes, such as to fund the building of St. Peter's. This mixing of spiritual realities (the effects an indulgence has on the soul) and temporal realities (paying alms to gain those good effects) did cause confusion sometimes. Indulgences were easily misunderstood by people and became a real problem when even churchmen misrepresented them—such as the Dominican Johann Tetzel (ca. 1465–1519), who was assigned by Albrecht to distribute indulgences throughout Germany.

Tetzel preached in town after town using what amounted to pocket-picking pitches. Come! he cried out. Come purchase an indulgence for your loved ones suffering in purgatory. Listen to their voices beseeching you! "As soon as the coin in the coffer rings, the soul from purgatory springs."[5] Luther's parishioners showed him the indulgences they had obtained and what they had seen and heard.

Angered, Luther was moved to act, and he was not the only one. His spiritual advisor Staupitz had already preached against indulgence abuses the year before. "The sound of the *gulden* which falls into the money chest will not free the sinner from sins," Staupitz said. The distributors did nothing but incite people to contribute, he thought, failing to instruct the people on what indulgences really were. In that sense, indulgences amounted to a "Roman pestilence," Staupitz charged.[6]

This was the context when Luther chose to challenge the practice through his *Ninety-Five Theses*. He did this on October 31, 1517, the day before All Saints' Day, when indulgence seekers would swarm Wittenberg's large relic collections. It seemed to Luther that these indulgence-seekers placed their hope too much in their indulgence receipts and in their works instead of interior faith. "They say, 'As soon as the coin in the coffer rings the soul from purgatory springs.' What 'springs' out is the spirit of avarice," he wrote (theses 27–28). "If the Pope knew the exactions of the venal preachers, he would prefer that the Basilica of St. Peter should lie in ashes rather than that it should be built out of the hide, flesh and bones of his sheep" (thesis 50).

Luther was not trying to start a reformation or a new church, but the fact that these outcomes resulted was not accidental. He did what many scholars did at the time in drawing up theses for debate. But he also took a step beyond this: he sent his theses to his Augustinian superiors and to church authorities. It seems he had them printed too, and copies in Latin and German circulated widely. They took on a greater significance than if he had merely posted them for public debate in Wittenberg.

Luther's ideas were vigorously debated throughout 1517–1519. Few suspected the world-transforming effects of these years. Knowledge of what resulted clouds the ability to understand the people of this time on their own terms. Many had longed for reform for generations. Various ideas of reform swirled around the late medieval period. It was not always clear where they would lead.

Many admired Luther's true genius and explication of scripture. Maybe he was a great reformer raised up by God? Erasmus had long advocated returning more deeply to scripture in order to reform theology and Christian life. That was why Erasmus defended Luther early on, wanting him to be heard and respected. Erasmus thought the value of simple faith and charity far exceeded the pursuit of fastidious external devotions. Along with Luther and others, he pushed against certain extremes of late medieval piety too.

Debating Church Authority

Luther's *Ninety-Five Theses* appealed especially to the German laity. They pointed out apparent financial abuse and expressed common grievances. Souls were not saved by indulgences and external works mediated by the clergy but by faith in the grace of God, free to anyone. That was a message that appealed widely in Germany at that time.

Within less than a year, Luther was a celebrity and a household name. At the same time, legal proceedings in church courts started against him. Prince Frederick of Saxony (1463–1525), who governed Wittenberg, guarded his prized professor and insisted no one drag him off to Rome. That is why Luther met with Cardinal Thomas Cajetan on German soil. The encounter grew heated, and Cajetan admonished Luther to recant or face the consequences. However, many of Luther's university colleagues admired and encouraged him. His students rallied around him. He constantly received reports on how well his writings sold. He believed his reform movement was both very *German* and very *young* (because of strong support from the younger generation). It seemed the way of the future.

Nevertheless, the brilliant German theologian Johann Eck (1486–1543) at the rival university in Ingolstadt in southern Germany attacked Luther. This bothered the reformer because Eck was German and young too—three years younger than Luther's thirty-five years. Eck *ought* to support Luther and his allies in the cause! Instead, Eck challenged Luther's views and longed to debate him.

This finally happened at Leipzig in 1519. Armed students traveled with Luther to protect him during the event. The city hired guards to watch over Eck. The audience swelled with abbots, counts, knights, and both the learned and the unlearned. The debate began after early morning Mass together. Two notaries recorded what was said, as did members of the audience.

The opening topic between Luther and Eck was whether the papacy was established by God or man. Luther argued Christ was the head of the Church and that various Church Fathers had not accepted the primacy of the pope. He thought the papacy was a humanly devised institution that had evolved over the centuries. The Eastern Orthodox Christians did not acknowledge the papacy as divinely established, for example. While he did not deny the duty of obedience to the pope, Luther implied the papal office was relatively unimportant. After all, the unity of Christendom was preserved even under the multiple claimants to the papacy during the Great Western Schism. Luther was quick and articulate and able to cite texts by memory. One eyewitness praised his knowledge and his affability but also noted that "everyone chides him for the fault of being a little too insolent in his reproaches."[7]

Eck was also very skilled. He agreed Christ was the head of the Church but defended the position of the Roman pontiff as Christ's vicar on earth based on scripture and the Church Fathers. He immediately accused Luther of agreeing with the teachings of John Wycliffe and Jan Hus, both of whom had been condemned by the Church as heretics. This ignited debate over which propositions of Hus were condemned. Eck defended the Council of Constance's decision against Hus.

Luther had a different view of Hus. He thought Hus held to many Christian truths. Staupitz and other Augustinians had come to believe that Hus had been unjustly condemned and wrongly burned at the stake. Luther switched from speaking in Latin to German. "I am being misunderstood by the people," he said. "I assert that a council has sometimes erred and may sometimes err. . . . Councils have contradicted each other, for the recent Lateran Council has reversed the claim of the councils of Constance and Basel that a council is above a pope." He asserted neither a council nor a pope can establish articles of faith or practices that were not found in the scriptures (such as indulgences). Therefore, "for the sake of Scripture we should reject pope and councils."[8]

The fallout from the Great Western Schism had confused Christians about the question of Church governance. Conciliarism claimed councils were above popes, and its influence was still felt in Luther's time. Luther's claim that the decision of Constance and Basel was reversed by Lateran V was based on a misunderstanding. No pope had accepted the decree of Constance and Basel that councils were above popes. There was no "reversal" as Luther claimed. Luther assumed the episcopal college could make a binding decision on Church governance even when deprived of its head, the pope. This was not the case and is not the case today. The pope and bishops must be in union, acting as one body. Today, it is clear in canon law that "the relationship of pope and college of bishops is based on the relationship the Lord established between Peter and the other apostles." In an age when that relationship seemed confused, Luther stood by the only position that seemed safe: "A simple layman armed with Scripture is to be believed above a pope or a council without it."[9]

Eck counterattacked with a key question he repeated in several different ways: "Are you the only one who knows anything? Except for you is all the Church in error?" Luther's answer might be regarded as the moment he left the Catholic faith: "I am a Christian theologian," Luther began. "I am bound. . . to defend the truth. . . . I want to believe freely and be a slave to the authority of no one, whether council, university, or pope. I will confidently confess what appears to me to be true."[10]

By this point, Eck had forced Luther to admit he was in league with a known heretic (Hus), and that he rejected the apostolic authority of councils and popes. Luther had followed his logic to its shocking end and clarified his position. Eck carried a large collection of Luther's heretical statements to Rome. He then helped draft the papal bull *Exsurge Domine* (1520) that threatened Luther with excommunication unless he recanted certain teachings.

Erasmus watched all this from a distance with growing apprehension. Luther and the tragedy unfolding around him would overthrow the peace of the Church and confound the cause of true reform for a long time. Erasmus wrote that through "unbridled impulse" Luther went beyond what was just. There was need for patience. The errors of the current age were great, but all ages have suffered from corruption. "Nor do I agree with those who say that the illness of this present time is too serious to be healed with gentle remedies," he wrote. Luther did not have to take this path to reform. Erasmus still hoped Luther would avoid discord, ruinous for all, and preach the pure Gospel for the "reformation of corrupt public morals."[11]

However, Luther chose to force the principle of reform over and against the principle of authority. This unintentionally contributed to much discord about the very nature of Christian revelation. In response to the bull *Exsurge Domine*, Luther gathered with colleagues and students in Wittenberg to burn it publicly, along with copies of canon law and various works of scholastic theology. Luther parted company from the approach of his old mentor Staupitz. Though the two men shared a common analysis of the troubled situation of the Church and of the Renaissance popes, Staupitz did not reject the papacy altogether as Luther did.[12] This was the dividing line between what would become the Catholic and the Protestant Reformations.

The Emergence of Protestant Reform Ideas

Luther was not burned at the stake as a heretic due to a unique set of political and cultural circumstances. The German-speaking lands were a complex patchwork of free cities and countless territories—some ruled by nobility and others by clergy. The lines between church and state were always a bit hazy. The Holy Roman emperor supposedly governed the whole, but his authority was severely limited. Rulers like Frederick of Saxony easily defied him and protected Luther. Political decentralization worked to Luther's benefit.

Luther's writings and his image circulated widely, thanks to the printing press. Poems celebrated him. Student riots burned anti-Luther works. He had become a German national hero. "The case is tending toward a greater crisis than certain men suppose," Erasmus wrote late in 1520.[13]

Throughout that year, Luther wrote a series of explosive texts laying out his view for reform. They were published in German for wide distribution and marked his complete break with Rome. He called his opponents "Romanists" to underscore the anti-foreigner appeal of his proposals to his German audience and to undercut the universal claims of papal supporters. *An Address to the Christian Nobility of the German Nation* advanced Luther's version of the "priesthood of all believers," which undermined the authority of the Church. "If we are all priests," he wrote, "why should we not also have the power to test and judge what is correct or incorrect in matters of faith?" Rome was a cesspool of money-grubbing, lying, robbing, harlotry, and contempt of God propped up by falsehood (Luther had read about the fake Donation of Constantine earlier that year). No wonder the Romans feared a reformation and a free council. Based on this alarmist thinking, he advocated "the Christian nobility should set itself against the pope as against a common enemy and destroyer of Christendom, and should do this for the salvation of the poor souls who must go to ruin through his tyranny."[14] Rather than seek reform within the institution of the Church, Luther turned to the state.

In one way, Luther's appeal to the princes was nothing new in the history of reform. Political rulers had long led such efforts, like Ferdinand and Isabella in Catholic Spain who in effect created a national church. The monarch of France had also created a national church at the expense of papal administrative authority with the Concordat of Bologna in 1516, gaining the right to choose and tithe the clergy. The German national church Luther envisioned, however, would push further in the cause of reform by allowing priests to marry, ending masses for the dead, and halting feast days, pilgrimages, and the cult of the saints. In other words, government influence would affect not just church administration but also important disciplinary and doctrinal changes.

This development marked an important moment in the history of church-state relations. As one historian noted, the medieval situation of states interacting with the *Church* was very different than the new situation of states interacting with *churches* in the Age of Reformations. "Struggles over the public exercise of power *within* the framework of the faith's teachings, practices, and institutions became public struggles over what the faith *was*, in print, from pulpits, and on battlefields." Erasmus wrote in 1527: "I foresee a violent and bloody century." He was tragically right.[15]

But Luther suspected nothing of that future. In his *Babylonian Captivity of the Church*, Luther laid out his vision of "evangelical" (gospel) reform against the "Romanists." Rome was the new "Babylon," the corrupt and tyrannical city that prevented God's people from truly believing and worshipping. "To begin with, I must deny that there are seven sacraments, and for the present maintain that there are but three: baptism, penance, and the bread," he wrote. Luther soon dropped the sacrament of penance as well. He appealed to unaided intellectualism to justify his position: "I shall tell you now what progress I have made as a result of my studies on the administration of this sacrament [Eucharist]. . . . I shall freely speak my mind, whether all the papists laugh or weep together."[16]

Another of his revolutionary works of 1520 was *On Christian Freedom*. "A Christian is a perfectly free lord of all, subject to none," he wrote. This treatise was a rhetorical masterpiece and laid out Luther's central vision of redemption. He wrote that no external thing has any influence on Christian righteousness. "One thing, and one thing only," is necessary for Christian life and freedom: "the most holy Word of God." Therefore, the soul "is justified by faith alone and not any works." Luther argued that the slavery of external works has nothing to do with the inner man. Christ does all. "Good works do not make a good man," he wrote. His qualification "but a good man does good works" did little to explain the importance of right action in the way of salvation.[17]

Luther's writings spread everywhere. They inspired others, including laymen, to publish pamphlets further explaining the new ideas to a wide audience. Luther and his associates had no control over this literature. As with internet news today, popular pamphlets used simplification and polarization to convey their message: the Roman Church is a powerful and corrupt institution that people can free themselves from by embracing the Gospel. Satirical cartoons appeared for the first time in history as a medium of dissent to hasten Luther's new idea of reform.

Reception of Luther's Idea of Reform

As Luther's ideas spread, Church authorities grew concerned. How should they deal with the situation? The answer was not clear. It was not even obvious in the early 1520s whether someone was a Catholic or a follower of Luther.

For example, thirty miles from Wittenberg at Torgau, the local bishop examined a Franciscan friar in 1522. The friar was preaching against indulgences and papal authority, and the dialog between them has been preserved to history:

"Listen you," the bishop said. "People are saying about you, that you want to start a new faith in Torgau with your preaching."

"Gracious Lord, I hope not," the friar answered.

"What have you been preaching about?"

"Gracious Lord, I don't know how to preach anything but the Word of God and the Gospel," the friar answered. The bishop then asked him why he had let his tonsure grow. He responded that it did nothing for him.

"How is someone supposed to see that you are a priest?" the bishop asked.

"From my words and deeds, and not from my clothes and tonsure," he replied. The bishop commented that he sounded Hussite and "Lutherite." He asked the friar what he thought about the Church.

"I believe any common gathering of Christians, whenever they come together, is the holy Christian church." The bishop asked him what he thought of ordination. The friar responded he did not believe in it unless ordination was proven from scripture. "Show me where it is written" was the phrase the friar used.

A theologian accompanying the bishop then tried to prove from Martin Luther's own writing that the apostles were ordained. The friar interrupted this line of reasoning: "I don't have anything to do with Doctor Martin [Luther]. I stand here for myself alone and want to answer for myself." The bishop then forbade him to preach. The friar said he would obey and left the scene. Then the bishop changed his mind and said to an attendant, "Go ahead, tell him he can still preach, as long as he can answer for it."[18] This example of hesitant ecclesiastical response shows how different ideas of reform mixed and could develop in any number of directions in the early 1520s.

Translating the Bible

Martin Luther was summoned before Emperor Charles V in 1521 at the Diet (Assembly) of Worms to recant or reaffirm his new teachings on scripture and on the nature of the Church. Pressed to speak clearly, Luther uttered some of the most momentous words in the history of Christianity: "Unless I am convicted by Scripture and plain reason—I do not accept the authority of popes and councils, for they have contradicted each other— my conscience is captive to the Word of God. I cannot and will not recant anything, for to go against conscience is neither right nor safe. God help me, Amen."[19]

Some accounts added the phrase "Here I stand; I cannot do otherwise" at the end, even though those words do not appear in the official transcripts. Whether Luther uttered them or not, the phrase "Here I stand" has ever afterward been associated with him and this pivotal moment. Luther's opposition of scripture to Church authority was so radical that he barely escaped arrest. With his words at Worms, historian Mark Noll observed, Protestantism was born.[20]

After this event, Luther was "kidnapped" by Frederick of Saxony to rescue him from being hunted down. Luther lived in exile at the remote castle of Wartburg. He translated the New Testament into German and penned letters, commentaries, treatises, and other translations, engaging his reformation movement through writing, the only way he could.

Luther's German New Testament was published in 1522. Thanks to the printing press, it spread widely and influenced the development of the modern German language. Luther urged everyone to pray to God for a right understanding of scripture. He hoped his translation would benefit the Christian world.

In addition, he dismissed critics of his translation, especially "papist" critics who did not understand the German language, the language of the people, from within as he did. Translation was both an art and a science, he wrote. One criticism levied against him was that Luther added the word "alone" to Romans 3:28: "So now we hold, that man is justified without the help of the works of the law, alone through faith" (Luther Bible). Luther justified his addition by arguing the word "alone" better conveyed the "sense of the text." To those papists who complained, he advised readers in his "Open Letter on Translating," say simply this: "Dr. Martin Luther will have it so . . . and he says that he is a doctor above all the doctors of the pope."[21]

Due to Luther's theological attachments, he did not believe all the books of the Bible were equally authoritative. He rejected seven books of the Old Testament as nonscriptural. In his *Preface to the New Testament* (1522), Luther highlighted John's gospel, Romans, Galatians, and Ephesians among a few others as the most necessary books of the Bible. St. James's epistle contained the verse most challenging to his *sola fide* theology: "So faith by itself, if it has no works, is dead" (Jas 2:17). This was why Luther wrote, "St. James' Epistle is really an epistle of straw." Therefore,

"I cannot put him among the chief books," though there are many good sayings in him."[22]

YOU BE THE JUDGE:

Didn't the Catholic Church make up which books were in the Bible during the Council of Trent?

The books of the Bible were long established before the Council of Trent. The council dogmatically defined the canon because it had been called into question when Martin Luther removed the seven Deuterocanonical books from the Old Testament scriptures in his translation. In his opinion, they were not divinely inspired. The Church often does not define dogma in a council until there are heretical teachings necessitating it.

The Deuterocanonical books were included in the Septuagint, a Greek translation of the Hebrew scriptures made in the third and second centuries BC. This translation was then used by the New Testament writers and the apostolic fathers of the Church. In fact, there are at least three hundred quotations from the Septuagint found in the New Testament, including references to the Deuterocanonical books.[23]

St. Jerome was commissioned in AD 382 at the Council of Rome to translate the approved canon of scriptures into Latin, creating what is known as the Latin Vulgate. Both the Septuagint and the New Testament canons, seventy-three books in all, were approved at this council, with later councils like Hippo (393), Carthage (397, 419), and Florence (1442) all ratifying this. These scriptures were accepted for centuries, until Luther denounced the seven books as apocryphal, or of doubtful authenticity.

Why did Luther remove these books? He wanted to "go back to the sources" and thought the Hebrew canon established by the Palestinian Jews in the late first century, several hundred years after the Septuagint, should be used instead. The Jews who created this new canon had rejected Christianity and had called the seven books into question because the original Hebrew versions of them could no longer be found. Later, with the discovery of the Dead Sea Scrolls in the 1940s, fragments of all the Deuterocanonical books were found (except for the book of Esther). Interestingly, many of the books Luther tried to cast doubt on contained evidence of teachings he later contradicted in his own teachings, like purgatory or the intercessory prayer of saints.

The Council of Trent decreed all seventy-three books of the Old and New Testament as sacred and canonical, resolving the discrepancies introduced by Luther's claims.

According to one commentator, the basis of faith for Luther was not simply the Bible. It was certain *parts* of the Bible that presented the Gospel as Luther understood it. These provided the lens for everything else. It was difficult to challenge Luther's interpretation even based on the Bible because of the subjective nature of his approach.[24]

The Radical Reformers

While Luther was in hiding, his colleague Andreas Karlstadt (1486–1541) in Wittenberg led the reform movement. He was a priest who possessed a doctorate in theology. Karlstadt enthusiastically supported Luther but had his own ideas as well, and he pushed for concrete reforms in Wittenberg. Monks and nuns began to leave their cloisters. Some married each other. Karlstadt was one of the first priests to decide to marry. Influenced by medieval mysticism, he advocated the inward testimony of the Holy Spirit—the *living* Word of God—as the highest authority.

Karlstadt argued material symbols could never convey spiritual benefits. Christians should stop using holy water and holy salt for spiritual purposes. They should seek the divine in an unmediated way. Erasmus had already written that if one embellishes a wooden or stone statue for the love of Christ, how much more should one privilege the writings that "bring Christ to us so much more effectively than any paltry image?" Karlstadt pushed this seeming conflict between the culture of image and the culture of text further. Images were contrary to the first commandment, he wrote. "Therefore, we should put them away in obedience to Scripture."[25] What can laypeople learn from pictures except to esteem the physical? Karlstadt believed images were tools of oppression by which Catholic clergy had kept the laity ignorant of scripture.

In response to this explosive message, student riots broke out in Wittenberg. They destroyed images, pulled down altars, and intimidated clerics as they said Mass. After these illegal acts, Karlstadt conducted a radically new evangelical communion service to replace the traditional Mass.

Three wandering preachers arrived in Wittenberg from Zwickau, a working-class town in a mining district ninety miles to the south noted for disparity and tension between rich and poor. They were all laymen. One was a weaver, one a former student at Wittenberg, and the third a blacksmith. These "Zwickau Prophets" claimed to have direct inspiration from the Holy Spirit. They began to preach that the end of the world was near. Christ's kingdom on earth should be established *now* by abolishing infant baptism, the Mass, Confession, images, relics, and all forms of oath taking. These ideas fit well with Karlstadt's. The prophets pushed further, insisting on the equality of human beings as the basis for sharing all goods in common. They thought the spiritual elect would ultimately rule the world.

The combined influence of Karlstadt and the Zwickau Prophets led the common people to believe they had the right to take matters into their own hands if civil authorities refused to remove "idols" from the churches. Wittenberg cannot delay in conforming to God's word! A mob of Wittenbergers was so upset by delayed action against idolatry that they stormed the churches and destroyed many images. They believed God's law is above any human law or even neighborliness and resolved to force Wittenberg into the mold of a truly Christian city.

Even though he later embraced a more pacific reform agenda, Karlstadt created a revolutionary precedent for religious and social change. He was the second most published Protestant reformer in the early years after Luther. Karlstadt's spirit would haunt the Age of Reformations and beyond.

By Whose Authority?

At this point, Luther called for a halt. The mayhem in Wittenberg shocked him so much he returned from exile to try to exert leadership and reclaim his more conservative idea of reform. All the old rituals and symbols were reinstated, and any remaining images protected. He condemned Karlstadt's influence in a series of fiery sermons. Even though both scholars appealed to the scriptures, Luther declared Karlstadt's teachings the work of the devil. He branded Karlstadt and the Zwickau Prophets as *Schwärmer*, meaning "fanatics" or "madmen." They claimed greater access to the Holy Spirit than the apostles, Luther wrote, but they merely "prowled about and flung around their shit."[26]

Germany was teeming with different visions of reform during the years 1517–1525. There were complex forces mobilized across the land working against the status quo. They sprang from the same popular discontent that fueled enthusiasm over Luther and anarchic resistance to authorities of all kinds, civil and ecclesiastical.

The conflict between Luther and Karlstadt involved different *herme-neutical* (interpretive) principles for understanding the scriptures. Luther tended to view the Bible through Paul's letters (his expertise) and the *sola fide* principle. Karlstadt adopted a "hermeneutic of transcendence," one historian summarized. Karlstadt emphasized God's radical otherness and the divorce between spirit and matter, leading him to condemn blessed salt, holy water, and holy images. In his literal approach to the scriptures, Karlstadt was also more concerned with social issues than Luther was.[27]

Luther was angry that Karlstadt had usurped his leadership while he was in exile. He claimed his interpretation of scripture over Karlstadt's. One opponent in Zwickau mocked Luther as "the German pope." Radical disagreements emerged as the central, tragic dynamic of the Protestant Reformations came into view for the first time. By whose authority was scripture interpreted, if not the traditional Church's? True, Eastern Orthodox Christians had not recognized papal authority for a long time. But they still recognized the apostolicity of their bishops and in that sense retained church authority. The Protestants wanted to ground everything on scripture. But whose interpretation of it? Without an answer to that question, the whole reform program fractured. Eventually, though, a certain consensus did emerge in the lived reality of Protestant culture.

The very principle of *sola scriptura* did not actually appear in the scriptures. Protestants often based it on the "doctrine of clarity." They held that scripture is clear, interprets itself, and can be easily read to understand the essentials of salvation. "You must realize," one Protestant theologian wrote about the Bible in 1537, "that I am not imposing purely human interpretations upon these passages, but basing my view entirely upon clear and definite Scripture."[28]

Catholics agreed with this doctrine of clarity to some extent. St. Peter Canisius (1521–1597), Doctor of the Church and effective Catholic catechist, met with Protestant leaders at the Colloquy of Worms (1557) to discuss their differences. He said that whenever the Bible really is clear and

distinct, "we gladly submit to its testimony and ask for no other authority or evidence." But as soon as conflict arises from its meaning and it
is difficult to decide on rival meanings, then we appeal "to the constant
agreement of the Catholic Church and go back to the unanimous interpretation of the Fathers."[29] Without this authority, heresy in matters of
fundamental Christian doctrine was unchecked.

To solve this problem, in practice Protestants often made implicit
appeals to other authorities than scripture. The "radical reformers" especially, such as Karlstadt and the Zwickau Prophets, often appealed to
one's inward sense of the Holy Spirit as the highest authority. As historian Brad Gregory wrote, this led to new confusions. Gregory stated that
it was rare for someone in a doctrinal controversy to say something like,
"You're right—I lack the Holy Spirit's guidance in my reading of Scripture,
and I see that you have it in yours. I admit I was mistaken, so I'll trust
you instead."[30] In questions of fundamental Christian doctrine, appeal to
one's inward sense of the Holy Spirit only increased the diversity of interpretations and encouraged the emergence of revolutionary movements.

One of the most widely read Catholic responses to these problems
raised by Protestant reform was by Johann Eck—the man who had debated
Luther at Leipzig in 1519. That debate shaped the trajectory of Eck's later
apologetical work, as seen in his most famous text, *Manual of Commonplaces against Martin Luther and His Followers* (1525). This work went
through ninety-one editions before 1600 and was a standard Catholic
handbook. The main issue in this "unhappy age of ours," he wrote, is that
Martin Luther put "his own judgment" above the "rule of faith which
the whole Church observes." In his first chapter on the "Church and Her
Authority," Eck quoted 1 Timothy 3:15, stating that the Church is "the
Church of the living God, the pillar and bulwark of the truth." He attacked
the idea that Jesus Christ had abandoned his bride the Church for one
thousand years, as Protestants claimed or implied. The Lutherans put the
scriptures above the Church. But they ended up causing new schisms and

fought "both among themselves and with others." Different Protestant groups disagree about the Eucharist, and they all claimed the scriptures as the basis for their teaching. "Who among them will be judge?" Eck asked. Christ did not write a book. But he did found a Church, and that Church was older than the sacred books his followers ended up writing. How does one even know what the Bible is apart from the Church? There is a consummate harmony between the holy scriptures of the Church and her councils.[31]

While debates such as these raged in print, a new threat moved in upon Luther—one far more serious than Karlstadt. He was a figure associated with the Zwickau Prophets, a man that Luther branded a fiend and a fanatic. He was the radical German theologian and revolutionary Thomas Müntzer (ca. 1489–1525), who believed resolutely he was led by the Holy Spirit against a godless world.

Reform Now! Revolutionary Apocalypticism

In the confusion of the 1520s in Germany, some believed they had a divine mandate to implement reforms in religion and society *immediately*. They advocated the "Reformation of the Common Man" through force if necessary.

One of these was Thomas Müntzer, who was a few years younger than Luther. He possessed a smattering of education from different universities and was ordained a priest around 1514. He met Luther in Wittenberg and shared his critique of indulgences. Luther recommended him for a church position in Zwickau. Deeply influenced by medieval German mysticism, by the end of 1521 Müntzer openly proclaimed his role as prophet of the end times. He insisted direct revelations from the Holy Spirit were a necessary addition to biblical authority: "All true pastors must have revelations." He prided himself on having better instruction in the Christian

faith than anyone he knew because he had *not* learned from "any monk
or priest." He knew the faith from within, contrary to the academic pre-
tension of people like Luther. He thought that while the faith he preached
differed from Luther's, "it is identical with that in the hearts of the elect
throughout the earth" who made up the spiritual church. "For anyone
who does not feel the spirit of Christ within him, or is not quite sure of
having it, is not a member of Christ, but of the devil."[32]

Müntzer made the fatal distinction between the "elect" and the "godless" as later Marxist and Islamist intellectuals have made in more recent
history. The difference between the elect and the godless for Müntzer
was not only an inner principle ("the spirit of Christ") but also a class
principle—an idea similar to Marx. The elect, Müntzer believed, was
always found among the poor and downtrodden. Those who lived com-
fortably and defended the status quo were the godless. There would be a
great clash between them and the elect. The sins of society were so great
that the princes needed to wield their swords against the godless and slay
them. When Luther condemned this violent approach to reform, Müntzer
attacked him in print as the "unspiritual soft-living Flesh in Wittenberg."
Luther had distorted scripture and "grievously polluted our wretched
Christian Church." He mocked him as a scholar and as "Dr. Liar." The
final judgment is near! Kill the godless. "Go to it, go to it, go to it! Show
no pity. . . . Pay no attention to the cries of the godless. They will entreat
you ever so warmly, they will whimper and wheedle like children. Show
no pity, as God has commanded in the words of Moses, Deuteronomy 7.
. . . Don't let your sword grow cold. . . . Hammer away ding-dong on the
anvils of Nimrod, cast down their tower to the ground."[33] (Nimrod was
the giant of medieval mythology who had supposedly built the Tower of
Babel.) Müntzer used the Bible to encourage violence. Such talk stoked
the fires of mass rebellion. It demonstrated the dangers of biblical interpretation separated from deep learning and the guidance of the Church,
as Pope Benedict XVI wrote in a 2010 post-synodal apostolic exhortation

about how to properly interpret violence in the Bible.[34] By Müntzer's words and deeds, the mystical element of religion broke away from the intellectual and institutional elements of religion, with terrifying consequences in the Peasants' Rebellion.

The Peasants' Rebellion

The German Peasants' Rebellion of 1524–1525 was the largest mass uprising in the history of Europe before the French Revolution. To this day its meaning is still debated. To Marxist historians, it was the Revolution of the Common Man and Müntzer was like a great communist visionary. In fact, Müntzer did establish a "communist" regime in one town and founded the Eternal League of God to spread uprisings even further. The peasants were angered by the erosion of their rights by the noble class, rights to hunting, fishing, collecting firewood, and grazing herds in common meadows. The peasants attacked castles and monasteries.

In addition to these worldly concerns, however, new reformation ideas also played a role. Preachers moved among the people drawing from Luther's idea of Christian liberty. The peasants demanded the end of serfdom: "Show us from the gospel that we should be serfs," they insisted.[35] They were convinced their demands were contained in the Word of God, and their interpretation was beyond questioning. They appealed to *sola scriptura* as their highest authority.

What was Luther's role in this uprising? He condemned the rebellion, but the leaders appealed directly to the Word of God to justify their demands in very Lutheran-sounding language. Luther penned his most controversial text in 1525: *Against the Robbing and Murdering Hordes of Peasants*. He wrote the rebels were destroying and taking property that was not theirs, turning everything upside down. "Let everyone who can, smite, slay, and stab, secretly or openly, remembering that nothing can be more poisonous, hurtful, or devilish than a rebel."[36] Whether the nobles read Luther or not, this is what they did. They killed around one hundred thousand poorly armed farmers and peasants. After claiming a rainbow was a sign of God's favor, Müntzer led an attack in 1525 in which more than five thousand peasants were killed in a single day. He was captured and executed.

Luther considered this a fitting end and something of a blessing. By siding with established authorities over the common man, however, Luther made himself and his reforms less attractive to many people. These critics denounced Luther's *Against the Robbing and Murdering Hordes of Peasants* for advocating the merciless slaughter of innocent peasants. Luther shot back that the peasants were not innocent, they were guilty rebels. "If you are going to read books this way [selectively]," "and interpret them as you please, what book will have any chance with you?"[37]

Another Reformation by the Book

Meanwhile in Switzerland, the Reformed tradition emerged as a Protestant alternative to Luther. The priest Ulrich Zwingli (1484–1531) took the lead. Historians often treat his reformation after Luther's—even though it started around the same time—because it developed more slowly and affected a smaller area at first. Ultimately, after John Calvin joined it, the Reformed tradition would affect the world much more than Luther's did. Calvin's theological systematization in his *Institutes of the Christian Religion* (1536) and the example of his church administration in Geneva built a strong foundation that eventually made major Reformed inroads in France, the Netherlands, Hungary, Scotland, England, the North American colonies and (much later) outside the West in places like South Africa and South Korea.

Zwingli was born in the beautiful Toggenburg valley in Switzerland into a hardworking, independent-minded peasant family. They were as devout as they were civic minded: three boys became priests; and two girls, nuns.

Two early factors seemed to shape the direction of Zwingli's idea of reform: his studies at the University of Basel and his reading of Erasmus. Basel was a center of humanistic learning in northwest Switzerland. While pursuing a master's degree, Zwingli embraced the humanist principle to return *ad fontes* in the Greek text of the New Testament. He also encountered Florentine Neoplatonism at Basel. This line of thought had developed out of the reintroduction of Plato's texts to Europe in the mid-1400s. It tended to stress the superiority of the spiritual over the material. This dichotomy would deeply influence Zwingli and the Reformed tradition.

The second formative influence on Zwingli was Erasmus. Around 1515, Zwingli read a poem by Erasmus called "The Complaint of Jesus." In the first person, Jesus complains he is bored in heaven because no one ever prays directly to him, only to the saints. The way Zwingli read the poem led him to a simple conclusion: discard not only the saints but also anything that comes between the believer and Jesus Christ. This central insight drove forward his reform, just as Luther's central insight into justification through faith alone drove his. The push for unmediated access to God led Zwingli into a total break with the past and with medieval Catholic piety. It also implied one did not need the Church. In this way he, too, arrived at the principle of *sola scriptura*.

Zwingli's idea of reform proved attractive. He preached at Einsiedeln in central Switzerland, a major pilgrimage center due to the presence of an image of the Virgin Mary associated with miracles. His message was "Christ alone saves." Christ can do so anywhere. Grace is not localized at specific points like pilgrimage sites. Zwingli also began to preach against a local indulgence distributor, and the bishop backed him. The historian Eire pointed out this showed how the medieval Catholic Church was in no way monolithic and could indeed absorb criticism.[38] Church leaders themselves had grave concerns over the way indulgences were handled. Many were concerned about reform. Luther and Zwingli's criticisms did not automatically lead to a break with Rome. Far from being censured by the Church, Zwingli was invited to apply for the prestigious position of "people's priest" at the most important church in Zurich in northern Switzerland. Since the other candidate had a concubine and six children, Zwingli was chosen. He began his duties there in 1519 at the age of thirty-five.

Zwingli's Zurich

The young priest was an electrifying preacher. His huge audiences absorbed his central message: the scriptures should be the ultimate measure of all church reform. His ideas came to resemble those of Karlstadt more than of Luther. By 1522, the year Karlstadt sparked violent change in Wittenberg, things began to happen in Zurich too.

Zwingli attacked what he considered nonbiblical religion, especially images and the Mass. He secretly got married, believing mandated celibacy was unscriptural. He defied the local bishop and—just as Luther had done—he asked civil authorities for protection.

Obligingly, the Zurich government called for a public disputation in 1523 on religious reform. It insisted that the Bible be the only authority on such questions. That premise disadvantaged the Catholics. Zwingli said, "I am confident and indeed I know, that my sermons and doctrine are nothing else than the holy, true, pure gospel, which God desired me to speak by the intuition and inspiration of His Spirit." There is another Church, he claimed, "which the popes do not wish to recognize; this one is no other than all right Christians, collected in the name of the Holy Ghost. . . . That church does not reign according to the flesh . . . but depends and rests only upon the word and will of God. . . . That Church cannot err." The Bible is so clear it made those who follow it infallible. Zwingli won, and this disputation marked the legal break between Zurich and the Catholic Church.[39]

Workmen removed the artistic treasures amassed in Zurich's churches over the centuries: crucifixes, holy water fonts, communion vessels, relics, votive lamps, vestments, organs, and carved choir stalls. Masses and sacred music ceased. Zurich was now a godly city! Zwingli rejoiced. "The Word alone and the words of the minister and the congregation reverberated in the vast, whitewashed, ritually clean spaces [of the churches], echoing the pure gospel," Eire wrote. Zwinglian reform spread across much of Switzerland, igniting episodes of violent iconoclasm. This was the beginning of a reformation that would transform the world in ways that Martin Luther had never imagined.[40]

Spiritual Transcendence

Zwingli's God was radically transcendent over his creation and wanted to be worshipped without material mediation. Luther did not separate matter and spirit in the way Zwingli did. Unbelievers seek mere created realities, Zwingli charged, but true believers go directly to God. He wrote that "whatever binds the senses diminishes the spirit." In an argument with Luther about the Eucharist, Zwingli hinged his spiritual interpretation on John 6:63: "It is the Spirit that gives life, the flesh is of no avail; the words that I have spoken to you are Spirit and life." He thought this was plain and simple. Christ could not have meant literally eating his flesh in John chapter 6. That would be an affront to God's transcendence. "The soul is spiritual, the soul does not eat flesh. Spirit eats spirit."[41] He thought the Eucharist had merely symbolic importance.

Zwingli's separation of spirit and matter demonstrated the influence of the Neoplatonic metaphysics (spirit over matter) in his education that was antithetical to traditional, incarnational Christianity. Zwingli implied God's transcendence was that of a great spiritual being spatially separate from the world. God was in heaven, man here on earth.

But what if God is *so* transcendent, in the Catholic view, so beyond all spatiality, that he can be present *in and with* his material creation? God is not "a being;" God is the very basis of being itself. Zwingli's philosophical training led him to overlook passages in the scriptures where matter mediated the spiritual, such as when Jesus used mud and water to heal a blind man (Jn 9:6–7), when people sought to touch the hem of Jesus's garment to be healed (Mt 14:36), and when handkerchiefs and aprons that had touched Paul were taken away to heal people (Acts 19:12). God is not in competition with the world or "contaminated" by matter. As C. S. Lewis wrote, God "likes matter. He invented it."[42] This is why Catholics hold that Jesus can be physically present in the Eucharist under the appearance of bread and wine: "he who eats ['gnaws' or 'chews'—from the Greek] my flesh and drinks my blood has eternal life, and I will raise him up at the last day" (Jn 6:54).

For Zwingli, God is spiritual and right worship of him alone leads to the right ordering of society. Religion was a total way of life, integrating individual with community. This is why right behavior mattered much more to Zwingli than to Luther, and the central goal of the Swiss reformers was to turn all citizens into good Christians. Whereas Luther adopted a "two kingdom" theology that accepted imperfection in the world, Zwingli and his associates aimed for perfection—both personal and communal. Sin could be controlled by the state, which in fact has the duty to suppress it in order to reveal the kingdom of God.

This did not lead to theocracy. In Zwingli's vision, the church and state would cooperate as a sacral community to create laws in accord with the Bible, regulate marriage, and supervise social charity. In practice, however, the state ran the church. Zwingli demonstrated high confidence in the ability of political control to build a true Christian community. By 1530, the new state church in Zurich made Sunday churchgoing a legal obligation. Citizens would be reformed whether they wanted it or not.

The Anabaptists

Zwingli dealt with dissent from his interpretation of the scriptures even more vigorously than Luther. From within his inner circle and among his earliest followers emerged a rebel. Felix Manz (ca. 1498–1527) protested that Zwingli's break with Catholicism had not gone far enough. He had shared Zwingli's critique of Catholicism but came to believe Zwingli compromised too much with the civil powers, watering down true Christian faith that ought to be radically based on the scriptures. The church should not mix with the world. The church should conform *in every way* to the model of the New Testament, including voluntary membership. This was why Manz and his followers believed only adults should be baptized because only they could make a conscious choice to believe. Thus, they were called "Anabaptists," or "re-baptizers."

Zwingli and the authorities of Zurich sensed danger. Manz's views undermined the medieval idea of the church as coextensive with society, including everyone automatically as a member just by living in a certain place. This "territorial church" idea gave baptism of infants both civil and religious functions, which Manz challenged. Zwingli could not tolerate such radicalism, even though each man justified his position with scripture. Manz was deemed a heretic by the Zurich authorities and was executed in 1526. He was the first Protestant to be killed by other Protestants.

Manz represented the third major branch of Protestantism alongside the Lutheran and the Reformed (Zwingli) that we first met in Karlstadt and Müntzer. This third branch has been called the "Radical Reformation" because it called for extreme application of *sola scriptura* and could provoke extensive social change. There were many different branches of the Radical Reformation that emerged in various places areas around Europe, ranging from pacifists to violent apocalypticists and spiritualists. Their unifying idea was opposition to the "Magisterial Reformation" (Luther and Zwingli) that cooperated with civil magistrates toward reform. The radicals saw church-state alliance as an unbiblical compromise. The Amish, Hutterites, and Mennonites are direct descendants of the Radical Reformation. Other traditions—such as the Baptists—have taken inspiration from it.

John Calvin (1509–1564)

John Calvin was one of the great figures of the Magisterial Protestant Reformation. As a French humanist and lawyer, Calvin agreed with Luther and Zwingli that civil magistrates played important roles in reform. But Calvin was closer to Zwingli than to Luther on other matters. Calvin systematized the Reformed tradition that had emerged in Zurich, enabling it to eventually affect much of the world.

Like most of the other Protestant reformers mentioned so far, Calvin studied for the Catholic priesthood, though he was never ordained. His father secured a Church *benefice* connected to a cathedral for him. A benefice was sum of money to be paid to him for services to the cathedral, but since he was not a priest, he had to hire another priest to perform the services. He pocketed the rest of the money and used it to pay for his education. This was a widely accepted practice used for scholarship aid. Calvin did not renounce this income until after he had become Protestant. In other words, the generosity of the late medieval Catholic Church paid for the training Calvin needed to break away from that Church and build up his own.

Calvin hated his Catholic past, and he left very few autobiographical records about his conversion to the Reformed tradition. Nevertheless, one famous letter he wrote in response to Cardinal Jacopo Sadoleto (1477–1547), a humanist and a Catholic reformer, provides one of the most interesting exchanges between a Catholic and a Protestant during the Age of Reformations. The cardinal wrote a letter in 1539 to the people of Geneva who had accepted the Reformed tradition of faith, inviting them back to the Catholic Church. Sadoleto wrote as a pastor and as a broad-minded Christian humanist who had accepted the fact that abuses plagued the Church. However, he thought authentic Christian faith is received from Holy Mother Church, not from "new men" armed with scripture who invent "novelties."[43]

In his reply to Sadoleto, Calvin used the literary device of an imaginary character speaking a monologue on behalf of all those who had left the Catholic Church for the Reformed tradition. This character was perhaps representative of Calvin's own biography growing up Catholic and then leaving the Church. "I, O Lord, as I had been educated from a boy, always professed the Christian faith," Calvin wrote through the voice of his imaginary character. "But at first I had no other reason for my faith than that which then everywhere prevailed." The culture instilled into the minds of all, Calvin continued, that the investigation of God's word was better left to priests. Everyone else should simply subdue themselves in obedience to the Church. In addition, the common man lacked training in proper worship of God. (At this time, Catholic lay piety was not centered on participating in the Mass; those who attended often prayed quietly on their own.) This young man did not know the way of salvation, Calvin noted, or how to fulfill his Christian duties. Instead, he was taught to make many satisfactions to God for his sins through good works and pieties while his conscience remained ill at ease. As nothing better came along, he continued his life as a mediocre Catholic.

Then a very different form of doctrine started up through the Reformed preachers. "Offended by the novelty" of these doctrines, Calvin's imaginary character "lent an unwilling ear" and "passionately resisted." He was averse to the new teachers because of "reverence for the Church," at least at first. But when he listened further, he realized that his "fear of derogating from the majesty of the Church was groundless." The Reformed preachers were not trying to create a schism but to correct faults. They spoke nobly of their desire for Christian unity.

The preachers convinced Calvin's young man it was no new thing for "Antichrists" to occupy the place of pastors. They explained the papacy had arisen amid a world "plunged in ignorance and sloth." The Church had been infiltrated, they believed, and "true order" had perished. The "true keys" of the discipline of the Church had been altered "very much for the worse." One should turn away from the Church-gone-wrong and toward the original, true Church of earlier times. In Calvin's mind, the young man's decision to leave the Catholic Church was one not of schism but of loyalty. The Romanists and their popes had taken the Church into schism. A faithful remnant needed to soldier on by returning to an imagined traditionalism. They praised God for delivering them from abandoning the word of God and the true (Reformed) church.[44]

Calvin's letter was published and widely distributed. It testified to one of the main reasons people left the Catholic Church at the time and even today: their changing spiritual needs had not been met. The attraction of Protestant ideas of reform emerged amid the tragic failure of Catholic pastoral ministry and catechetics in an age of profound tension between oral and literate cultures. The old model wherein primarily the clergy were the educated class was changing. Rising standards of living, the spread of universities, the humanist appeal, and the printing press created new social conditions to which the old Church struggled to adapt.

This was partly why Calvin's letter won the day. Geneva turned its back on Cardinal Sadoleto's proposal to return to Catholicism. City leaders invited Calvin to come and help them create a godly city in the Reformed tradition.

The Protestant Rome

Calvin's response to Sadoleto revealed the psychology and spirituality of the early Reformed movement. The true church was restored! That belief led one Protestant commentator to ask rhetorically, "Do you know of any reason why Geneva ought not now call itself the true Church of God which has received and protected with all its power that which God first announced by His Prophets and later by His Son and the Apostles?"[45] Notice the break in historical continuity implied by this passage between the time of the Apostles and the present 1500s. Johann Eck, the great Catholic apologist in Germany, would have attacked the idea that Jesus Christ had abandoned his bride the Church for one thousand years.

Building on the ideas of *sola fide* and *sola scriptura*, Calvin added the concepts of election and predestination to express the idea that God predestines the elect for salvation from the beginning of time. He also added another *solus* (alone) at the heart of his idea of reform, *soli Deo Gloria*: "To God alone be the glory." One should not honor Mary, angels, or saints—only God.

YOU BE THE JUDGE:

Don't Catholics pray to the saints instead of Christ?

The simple answer is no! Catholics ask the saints for their prayers, much the same way you would ask a friend or family member to pray for you in a time of need.

The saints are owed a certain amount of reverence because of their closeness to God in heaven and the lives they lived while on earth. But they are created beings. The degree of reverence appropriate for them is derived from a classical Greek term: *dulia*. The type of reverence owed to God has a special character that makes it categorically different. After all, it is the worship that is offered to the uncreated Triune God of the universe! *Latria*, in Greek, refers to the type of worship, adoration, and veneration due to God and God alone.

What about the Virgin Mary? She is held in even greater esteem and venerated more devoutly than her saintly counterparts because she is the Mother of God. But she is not worshipped with adoration like God. She is understood to be a very special intercessor, one close to God who acts as a mediatrix by presenting human requests and prayers to him. The term *hyperdulia* is used to express the level of veneration owed to the Virgin Mary. It exceeds that of the saints (hyper is derived from Greek for "over" or "above") but is still fundamentally different than the adoration given to God.

The reverence given to the saints is what inspires the use of relics, pilgrimages to their graves, and devotions to them. Rather than thinking of these things as superstitious, Catholics understand them as expressions of friendship with persons in heaven who can help those in the Church on earth become closer to Jesus. The love of Christ the saints exhibited in their lives is a primer on what it takes to have a close, personal relationship with Jesus Christ.

As his vocation matured in Geneva, Calvin came to see himself as God's agent. Despite his dislike of ecclesiastical authority in the Catholic Church, he inaugurated a new and very strict system of ecclesiastical authority in Geneva. Calvin's goal was *not* to encourage everyone to interpret the scriptures for themselves. Genevans should interpret them as *Calvin* did. On this basis, he would help turn Geneva into a godly city set against the corruptions of Rome.

The *Ecclesiastical Ordinances* of 1541 gave Calvin and his clergy an exalted authority to govern Geneva alongside the magistrates. He insisted this arrangement reflected gospel precedent. All children had to be brought to churches for religious instruction. The church-city mandated attendance and attentiveness at Sunday sermons. It was illegal to arrive

late or to fall asleep during them. Through home visits, clergy checked
to make sure families lived morally. The consistory was formed by civil
leaders and churchmen as a kind of Genevan magisterium. It defined and
controlled morality and, like the Spanish Inquisition, punished offenders.
Blasphemy, adultery, and gossiping could lead to fines or imprisonment.
Theological differences with Calvin could lead to execution. Clothing was
regulated: no immodesty or extravagance allowed. Certain hairstyles were
codified as "un-Christian," as were certain names and parties with more
than twenty guests. Those attending secret Masses, or "Romish" festivals
or pilgrimages, could get into trouble. Rules were created to prevent con-
tamination in Geneva from the outside world, with innkeepers on the
front lines of reporting anyone entering the city who was suspected of
debauchery or of playing cards. This siege mentality led to censorship of
not only books but also correspondence. Calvin's reformation was relentless in its application of political force to render change. Geneva became
a center from which missionaries fanned out across Europe.

The Genevan model of reformation sought to link religion to every
facet of life. Its fundamental premise was there could be no compromise between idolatry and true religion. Around Europe, iconoclasts of
the Reformed tradition regularly broke into monasteries, convents, and
churches to destroy Catholic property—especially crucifixes, books, breviaries, and statues. Reformed leaders sought to suppress incertitude,
repress questions, and march forward toward the righteous "city on a
hill"—an idea transported to the Massachusetts Bay Colony in 1630 by
the Puritan John Winthrop. While Calvin himself did not advocate resistance to all idolatrous rulers, later Calvinist thinkers did so. They would
go on to say all rulers who tolerate idolatry forfeit their right to rule.[46] As
Calvinism emerged from within various European populations, it was no
wonder that many Catholics and Lutherans viewed it as seditious.

England: Slow Reform

What about England? Historians have long debated to what extent the people there welcomed departure from Catholicism after King Henry VIII broke away from the Church in 1534. Certainly, many parishes adapted easily. Protestant ideas of reform seemed to represent liberty and truth. Having access to the whole Bible and worship in English appealed to them. Other parishes did not adapt easily and resisted change.

The historian Eamon Duffy argued that Catholicism was strong in England before the Age of Reformations. By the late Middle Ages, laypeople there desired a more structured and elaborate prayer life, evidenced by the books they bought. Literacy increased during the 1400s. Scriptural prayer books sold well. They enabled people to say morning prayers, pray at Mass, secure indulgences, and meditate on the Passion of Jesus. There were pamphlets on the rosary, on dying well, and on pilgrimage sites. One could buy books on saints' lives, summaries of Old Testament stories, the gospels in various forms, and sermons, much of it in English. A major weakness, though, in the educational and devotional program of late medieval Catholicism in England was the ban on the English Bible as a whole, due to fear of the heretical Lollards.[47] Nevertheless, catechetics was adapting to changing conditions in the rise of lay demand for a deeper and wider spirituality. Lay Catholic humanists in England like lawyer St. Thomas More and bishop St. John Fisher continually emphasized the centrality of the Bible.[48]

YOU BE THE JUDGE:

Didn't the Church prohibit Catholics from reading the Bible?

This is a complicated question with several layers that require contextual understanding. First, the simple answer is the Church did not forbid Catholics from reading the Bible. She was, however, cautious about letting them read it without the teaching authority of the Church. The average individual in the Age of Reformations had very little theological training. The laity were terribly lacking in catechesis, though devotions and piety were strong (they had access to much of the scriptures in their devotional materials). Without the teaching authority of the Church to help them understand and elucidate scripture, and to correct any misconceptions, the general population was in danger of making serious errors that could affect their souls and communities. The Church even worried radical interpretations could cause violence, much like what happened with the Hussite Rebellion in the 1400s or the Peasants' Rebellion in Germany during the 1520s.

Second, before the invention of the printing press, books were rare, expensive to produce, and highly valuable. The handwritten copies of the Bible available to the (largely illiterate) public tended to be kept in the Churches, locked away or chained down so they would not be stolen. Did this mean the Church was keeping people from reading them? To the contrary, the Church was keeping them available to *all* the faithful by keeping them safe from thieves.

Third, when the Church later placed copies of the Bible on the Index of Forbidden Books, it was because they were Protestant versions that were missing the Deuterocanonical books (the seven books Martin Luther called apocryphal in the Old

Testament) or because they were a poor translation that could be damaging.

Fourth, the available Latin texts were accessible to those who were educated. If people were educated enough to read, they were generally also educated in Latin. Latin was still a commonly spoken, even universal, language until well into the seventeenth and eighteenth centuries. The need for vernacular texts only began to change during the sixteenth century.

Looking back, it seems the Church ought to have stepped in to solve the problem of the lack of education for the laity sooner rather than focusing so much on damage control. The average person did not have the time and leisure to study and learn enough to support their understanding of scripture, and they also did not have anyone who could teach them easily. The clergy also lacked education and were unable to offer much catechesis. People did not have spiritual leaders who could help them interpret the Bible. These were areas that called for reform.

The Church recognized these problems and noted the change of literacy levels too. The Council of Trent directly answered the needs of education for clergy, catechisms, and systematic ways to reach the laity. After seeing the Protestant reformers' use of pamphlets to spread their ideas, encouragement of vernacular translations, and defense of the "freedom" to focus on a personal approach to scripture, the need to catechize Catholics became very evident.

In the end, even Martin Luther, who originated *sola scriptura*, did not like its results when individuals started acting as if their own interpretation was the new standard, effectively setting up a new "tradition" to follow.

Nevertheless, despite official opposition, Lutheran ideas made inroads, particularly at Cambridge. The early, bottom-up influence of Luther's ideas (and later Calvin's) among certain sectors of the population appealed to *sola scriptura* as the highest authority in reform. On the other hand, the top-down, monarchical reform movement inaugurated by King Henry VIII appealed to royal authority in reform. In the background, Catholic resistance to both made the situation even more complex. The presence of several movements at once meant reform in England proceeded in fits and starts, slowly over decades.

The story of monarchical reform began with King Henry VIII, who reigned 1509–1547. Early in his reign he was zealous in his allegiance to the Church. Pope Leo X named him "Defender of the Faith" for writing against Martin Luther in 1521. Henry VIII heavily criticized Luther for persuading people to disobey the pope. "Truly, if any will look upon ancient monuments, or read the histories of former times, he may easily find, that since the conversion of the world, all churches of the Christian world have been obedient to the See of Rome."[49] The humanist Thomas More (1478–1535) felt it necessary to advise Henry against flattering the pope too much. Arguments such as these would appear highly ironic after Henry's later actions repudiating papal authority.

Up Close and Personal:
ST. THOMAS MORE

St. Thomas More's martyrdom is a pivotal moment in history that many have drawn strength and inspiration from but it sometimes overshadows his life of great virtue. His life enabled him to die for the truths of the Church—his conscience had been well formed in them. His courage in adhering to his conscience was remarkable.

Thomas More was born 1478 in London, England, the second of six children. His father, a lawyer and eventually a judge, provided an excellent education for his son, culminating at Oxford

University to study classics. More excelled in academics, though he had a deep attraction to the monastic life too. He spent a year in a Carthusian monastery after completing his studies in law, and it formed him deeply. He later integrated the monastic style of living into his married home life and fatherhood, with time for study, prayer, Mass, ascetic practices, and the same sort of peaceful and intentional approach to daily life found there. He educated his children well in the classics, both his sons and his daughters (though educating girls in this way was unusual for the time). He was close to his children. When they were older, they wrote letters to each other when they were apart.

His lively intellectual life was rooted deeply in the truths of the Church yet encompassed the ideas of the time too. Humanism had a great impact on him, as did his friendship with the Catholic biblical scholar Desiderius Erasmus. He met and engaged new ideas, but he recognized the dangers and heresies inherent in the Protestant Reformations. Jerome Williams' excellent book *True Reformers* notes More's concern with Martin Luther's attempts at reform precisely "because he thought Luther to be engaged in something other than reform. Having steeped himself in the early Church Fathers, More knew that the apostolic Church to which Lutherans appealed was very different from what they claimed."[50]

More was serving as chancellor of the Duchy of Lancaster when the Act of Succession passed and Henry VIII declared himself the supreme head of the Church of England, something More refused to recognize as true. (This was all prompted by Henry VIII's desire to divorce and remarry, and Pope Clement VII's refusal to annul the legitimate marriage.) More quietly resigned in 1532 yet was still met with pressure and imprisonment in an attempt to force him to sign an oath swearing to the act. He refused, but he also refused to speak openly about his thoughts on the entire matter. In fact, it was not until after his execution was ordered that More spoke his mind. Williams points out an important truth: More knew he could trust and follow his conscience because it had been well formed according to Church teaching. He was unmovable because he was grounded in the "universal testimony of the Church."[51] In his letters to his daughter, Margaret Roper, written during his imprisonment in the Tower of London, More made it clear he had done his due diligence: "Wherein I had not informed my conscience neither suddenly nor slightly but by long leisure and diligent search for the matter." He chose to align himself with eternal truths instead of political machinations of his time, writing, "I am not then bounden to change my conscience, and confirm it to the council of one realm, against the general council of Christendom."[52] Because he steadfastly clung to the truths of the Church, he was martyred. More is a stunning example when compared to other reformers who cited their consciences as justification for their revolutionary actions.

Interestingly, just as during the post–Vatican II era, issues of papal authority and sexuality drove dissent from the Church. Henry desired a male heir. His marriage with Catherine of Aragon (1485–1536), daughter of Spain's great Catholic monarchs Ferdinand and Isabella, had not produced one. Of the six children born between 1510 and 1518 (including two sons), only one child survived—a girl, named Mary. Henry became convinced this situation was a divine punishment because Catherine had been married to Henry's brother before he died. He came to believe his marriage with Catherine was immoral. He applied to Rome for an annulment, but the pope considered the marriage valid and denied it.

Henry was angry. He was also in love with Anne Boleyn (1507–1536), the sister of one of his former mistresses. He resolved to find a solution. Two courtiers stepped up to help: Thomas Cromwell (1485–1540) and Thomas Cranmer (1489–1556). Cranmer had encountered Luther's ideas at Cambridge. Cromwell was a lawyer who worked with Henry to detach the English Church from obedience to the pope and make it a branch of government. He justified this based on conciliarist assumptions about the limits of papal power and the strong role of princes in the Church. After Cranmer became archbishop of Canterbury, he annulled Henry's marriage to Catherine. Everything was finally moving Henry's way. He requested the Act of Supremacy (1534) from Parliament to declare himself and his successors "the only supreme head on Earth of the Church of England." This marked the official break from Rome and in effect made Henry "king-pope" in England.

Assisted by Cromwell and moved by greed, Henry disbanded the nation's monasteries, convents, and friaries between 1536 and 1541, transferring vast amounts of property to the crown. This was one of the greatest revolutions in English history. It hurt the poor across the entire land by closing the very institutions most concerned with the poor. Monastery infirmaries, for example, which provided shelter for the aged, the sick, and the hurt, nearly ceased to exist. Henry spent much of the money he raised from selling Church properties on war with France during the 1540s.

The Dissolution of the Monasteries was a large step toward Protestantism. At the same time, Henry VIII was no Protestant reformer. Even as the monks and nuns left their former lives, Henry blocked Protestant influence. Most Catholic images stayed in place. Parliament's Six Articles (1539) defended the real presence of Jesus Christ in the Eucharist, priestly celibacy, and auricular confession. Henry's government executed *both* Catholics loyal to Rome *and* Protestants of the Anabaptist persuasion. Many Protestants fled the country and happened to end up in Reformed cities rather than Lutheran ones, which would lead eventually to Calvin having more influence in England than Luther.

The Voices of Morebath

How did all this affect the English people? Events in the tiny sheep-farming village of Morebath in Devonshire in southwest England reveals how the path to Protestant reform in England was by no means straightforward.

The only priest in Morebath was named Christopher Trychay (pronounced "Tricky"). Remarkably, this pious and devoted pastor kept a record of parish life between 1520 and his death in 1574. It showed how a close-knit, self-contained rural community handled religious change over the key decades of transition. This parish suffered from financial woes and interpersonal strife, but the Catholic piety of its people emerges through the pages of Trychay's record. During the reign of Henry, Catholic parish life continued largely undisturbed, even as local monastic life came to an end. It was during the reign of Edward VI (1547–1553), son of Henry VIII, that things changed. Edward was very young. Thus, powerful men around him with overtly Protestant reform ideas gained the upper hand at the English court. Iconoclasm and hatred of all things Catholic increased. Morebath parishioners hid their priest's vestments to prevent confiscation by the king's inspectors.

During Edward's reign, changes in worship and ritual affected Catholics at the level of everyday life. Many in western England became uneasy and angry. Twenty-five miles south of Morebath at the village of Clyst St. Mary, for example, a small but telling incident occurred in 1549. Walter Raleigh, father of the famous explorer by the same name and a staunch supporter of Protestant reform, was riding along one day. He overtook an old woman on her way to Mass. She was praying as she walked, holding rosary beads in her hand. He challenged her, asking what she meant by carrying such illegal beads. He threatened her with prosecution. The woman hurried to the church where parishioners were gathering for Mass. She told them of the man's aggressions. Enraged, they nearly lynched

Raleigh, burned a local mill, and escalated the rebellion that was already spreading across the region.

This was just one example of what motivated the Prayer Book Rebellion of 1549. The larger issue was the redefinition of the beliefs and rituals of the Mass by the new *Book of Common Prayer* mandated by the government that year, which tried to suppress notions of sacrifice and transubstantiation. Gone were many of the ancient prayers, litanies, and rubrics. Pockets of resistance emerged, like at Clyst St. Mary, sparked by the rosary episode. Tragically, that same village was the later scene of a pitched battle in which hundreds of peasants were killed by royal forces. Clyst St. Mary was burned to the ground. Their attachment to the rosary and other sacramentals cost them dearly.

For a long time, scholars thought Morebath (situated just north of Clyst St. Mary) simply took most of this change in stride as a peaceful, law-abiding village. However, in the late 1990s, the historian Eamon Duffy realized a mistranscription of Trychay's record had hidden a significant fact from historians: the parish participated in the Prayer Book Rebellion of 1549. After all, the parish's images and ritual furnishings were largely gone, its vestments concealed, and its parish organization dissolved. The people's patience with imposed reform snapped. Parishioners financed and equipped five young men to join the rebels. Though viewed as traitors from the government's perspective, the fighters from Morebath believed themselves to be honest men defending the traditions of their fathers and the well-being of their community.[53]

The rebellion failed. Three of Morebath's five young men did not come home. According to the law, the parish surrendered their Mass book and the great breviary used for singing Latin offices. The people had to buy another copy of the 1549 *Book of Common Prayer* because they had likely burned their first copy in protest. The costs of reformation were mounting. In 1552, they were forced to reveal the whereabouts of their hidden vestments.

Then King Edward died. Queen Mary came to the throne. She was the daughter of Henry VIII and his first wife, Catherine, and she was a staunch Catholic. Mary was determined to reverse the Protestant Reformation in England. She faced an incredibly difficult task, since Protestant reforms had already proceeded so far. Priests had married, churches had been stripped, and the monasteries were in ruins. Nevertheless, Trychay in Morebath rejoiced. "His parishioners rallied to the restoration of Catholicism," Duffy wrote.[54] An image of the Virgin Mary came out of hiding, as did many other paintings, books, and furnishings that used to be a source of communal identity.

However, Queen Mary made two serious mistakes. First, she decided to marry King Philip II of Spain, another strong Catholic who was hated by the English Protestants. Second, she started to hunt down and execute Protestants, earning herself the nickname "Bloody Mary." These choices motivated previously indifferent people against Catholicism in England.

When the Protestant supporter Queen Elizabeth came to the throne in 1558, her reversal of Mary's Catholic policies was welcomed by many. The new religious laws were strictly enforced. At Morebath, once more Trychay conformed to the new regime. The Mass book was hidden for safekeeping, and the parish bought the new communion book and other reformed texts. Vestments were hidden once more, and the interior of the church was stripped yet again.

By the 1570s, rapid change came to Morebath. The Thirty-Nine Articles as finalized in 1571 were the defining statement of doctrine and practice in the Church of England. They stipulated the scriptures were the sole rule of faith, that general councils may err, there were only two sacraments (baptism and the "supper of the Lord"), that priests may marry, and that "the bishop of Rome has no jurisdiction in this Realm of England." This was all peacefully accepted in Morebath. The older generation who remembered the traditional ways had passed. As chalice gave way to communion cup, and the altar to a table, people's attitudes adjusted.

By 1573, the old priest Christopher Trychay expressed gratitude for the new religious order. He had conformed several times during his life. He was not one to rebel. Some priests had rebelled and were killed. Others had fled the country. As Duffy wrote, "It is hard to see what else such a man in such a time could have done." He was devoted to his place and his people amid the sheep pastures and dirt lanes of rural England. There was nowhere for him to be, Trychay decided, but among the people he had baptized, absolved, married, and buried for two generations, Duffy wrote.[55] England was slowly becoming Protestant.

YOU BE THE JUDGE:

Should Pope Pius V have excommunicated Elizabeth I of England?

Elizabeth I was raised and educated in a Protestant milieu. Despite taking an oath at her coronation to govern England as a Catholic country, she immediately started to restrict and persecute Catholics. She had little sympathy for her Catholic subjects. It was effectively illegal to be Catholic in England and to celebrate the sacraments when Elizabeth issued the Act of Uniformity in 1559 prohibiting the practice of the Catholic Mass. The act abolished papal supremacy and made defense of it punishable by loss of goods, imprisonment, or even death. Catholics were taken out of public office. They were required to attend the Church of England services or levied with steep fines if they refused.

Nearly a decade went by with Pope Pius V trying to reach out to her, hoping for her conversion and making attempts to support the Catholics of the country. After Pius's attempts bore no fruit, he decided his only option was to issue a bull of excommunication in 1570. This bull effectively nullified Elizabeth's sovereignty for her Catholic subjects, as well as levying serious charges like heresy against her.

Elizabeth's reaction to the papal bull entailed even more severe persecutions for them. Executions began. Great saints like St. Margaret Clitherow (1556–1586) suffered martyrdom because of heroic actions like hiding priests in their homes.

Some argue that since Elizabeth I was not even Catholic, the pope technically could not excommunicate her. So what was the pope trying to accomplish with the bull? He hoped to give persecuted Catholics the encouragement to stand against the abuse they had been enduring for years. The pope had little recourse to other methods of support for the Catholics of England. He had thought Spain and France would support the bull by suspending commerce with England if the bull were published there too. The pope hoped this would compel Elizabeth I to abdicate her throne without the need for violence. (Ideally her Catholic cousin, Mary Stuart, would take her place.) Unfortunately, the Spanish king did not agree, and Pius's hopes of support did not materialize.

Were Pius's actions good for the Catholics in England? The bull caused more suffering and persecution for them, and it added to a long-standing prejudice against Catholics in the country. But it also afforded the opportunity for integrity—to know that you could stand for truth and that the Church was standing beside you.

The Emergence of Protestant Culture

After 1560, much of northern and central Europe adhered to Lutheran, Reformed, or Radical Protestant churches. New forms of cultural life emerged there that increasingly diverged from the Catholic south.

Protestant devotions were centered on the household. They involved reading alone or aloud to others and prayer. Hymns provided musical outlet (Luther wrote many beautiful hymns). The popular Catholic culture of pilgrimages, festivals, and sacred dramas that revolved around extravagant Baroque churches contrasted greatly with the austere, cerebral religious life of hardworking Protestant tradesmen and shopkeepers who attended their bare meeting houses to listen to long sermons.[56] While all this encouraged literacy among the Protestants and art among the Catholics, it also made for mutually incomprehensible religious cultures dividing the continent for centuries.

The Protestant cultures of the north proved attractive to many people because they promised biblical religion through direct encounter with the scriptures, unmediated by a hierarchical Catholic clergy. This was the "pure" word of God and the true "spiritual religion," they believed. In reality, however, state-imposed ecclesiastical structures often channeled that "direct" encounter with the scriptures in predetermined directions.

Above all, there was the attraction of Protestant intellectualism in the new age of books. For the most part, Protestant reform movements had emerged from universities through university-trained men. They thought one advanced in Christian faith and holiness more through study than charitable works. Reading and writing functioned as pious exercises. This felt liberating—at least to the literate. Protestants pioneered Bible versification and catechisms in their definitive form—developments that benefited Catholics too. It seemed to Protestants in Britain that they defended learning while Catholics defended ignorance, with their mechanical rituals and popular devotions to saints and images. It was true that at this time, Catholics tended to emphasize works over words. They prioritized living virtuously, loving God and neighbor, and participating in the sacraments and the life of the Church over the ability to articulate the faith. Protestants sometimes acknowledged that Catholics had a greater reputation for personal devotion, and they regularly read Catholic books of devotion (such as *The Imitation of Christ* and *Introduction to the Devout Life*).[57]

Protestantism was a religion of the book. There was a certain paradox here for Reformed Protestants, in particular, for whom no material thing could be reverenced. Zwingli and Calvin had made that clear. Regardless, Protestant laity in Britain, for example, sometimes reverenced bibles as material objects. Opening bibles at random to point out phrases could be a form of divination. People wanted pocket-sized bibles to carry with them, sometimes even subscribing spiritual power to the physical thing itself. The Bible served as the sole sacred object in much of British Protestant culture. This marked the triumph of the new technology of printing and the literate world it enhanced.

Christopher Dawson pointed out that as Protestant and Catholic religious cultures developed, they did share certain characteristics. First, they both sought to recover moral discipline and activism amid the laxity of the Renaissance. Second, a tendency toward interiorization of religion and spiritual life marked both cultures. Third, they each retained respect for certain traditions of the Renaissance through the ideal of Christian humanism. It was Catholicism, however, that was better able to make use of Renaissance art, music, and architecture in the service of religion due to its intensely sacramental and liturgical character.[58] This artistic and sacramental impulse, along with great saints and Catholic scholars would propel the Catholic Reformation.

Chapter 3

Catholics

The Catholic Reformation

The late medieval longing for reform led to two different outcomes. On the one hand, many came to see the old Church as hopelessly corrupt. They thought the problem was deficient doctrine. Inhabiting an environment enthused by discoveries of new worlds and novel technologies, they sought fresh ideas of reform. They tried to restore what they thought of as the original church hijacked by Rome during the Middle Ages. After 1529, when several princes and independent cities issued a "Protestation" against the Holy Roman Empire, which had mandated Catholicism, they became known as "Protestants." Naturally, the various Protestant movements developed not only in reaction to Catholicism but also in reaction to each other, even though each thought of itself as based solely on the scriptures.

On the other hand, the late medieval longing for renewal led to reform *within* the Church through a distinctly Catholic idea of reform *in capite et in membris* (in head and in members). We have already seen some evidence of reform *in membris* prior to Luther in Spain and in the Netherlands. Catholic reformers held that the problem of corruption was not deficient doctrine but flawed people who failed to live the Christian life.

Up Close and Personal:

REFORMING RELIGIOUS ORDERS BEFORE THE COUNCIL OF TRENT

Many established orders, such as the Benedictines, the Augustinians, and the Franciscans, made efforts to reform in the early sixteenth century. In addition, there were several newly formed religious orders and efforts toward reform right before the beginning of the Protestant Reformations and the Council of Trent:

- Oratory of Divine Love in Rome (around 1514): Inspired by St. Catherine of Genoa, laymen and priests dedicated to a life of prayer and charitable works for the poor.
- Capuchin Order (between 1525 and 1528): This Franciscan order branched off in order to follow a stricter interpretation of the Rule of St. Francis. It was characterized by preaching, austere poverty, and service to the poor.
- Ursuline Order in Brescia, Italy (1535): Founded by St. Angela Merici, it was the first to focus on the education of young girls with the hope of renewing the family through vocations to motherhood. The order also focused on charitable works for the poor.

True reformers—the saints—recognized that deploring evil too much took away from the faith, hope, and charity needed to overcome it. Focusing on being "scandalized" in front of deficiencies simply justified one's desire to rebel. As the Catholic apologist St. Francis de Sales (1567–1622) wrote,

Protestant rebels had arranged for a divorce of sorts between Jesus Christ and his spouse the Church. Then they contracted a second and new marriage to a younger and seemingly more attractive woman. They did this in a self-appointed way, making them false prophets, de Sales charged.[1] The saints believed, by contrast, that the essential response to hardship and sin in members of the Church is not divorce but the call to conversion and union with Jesus Christ *through* his mystical body (the Church). In fact, the Church is a hospital for sinners, not a society of saints—even though there are also great saints who belong to it.

The Catholic Reformation had to respond to Protestant challenges at the level of theology, culture, and politics. Historians have traditionally referred to this as the "Counter-Reformation." Catholics *countered* the Protestants by emphasizing how they were unlike them. As one historian wrote, "Simply by surviving and thriving, Lutherans and Zwinglians and Calvinists and Anabaptists changed everything for Catholics, as they did for one another."[2] But Catholics did not simply oppose Protestants. They advanced their own reform movement too, independent of and prior to Luther. The "Counter-Reformation" was a particular mode of the broader-based "Catholic Reformation." The Catholic Reformation laid the foundations of modern Catholicism.

In the first stage of the Catholic Reformation before 1517, people such as Francisco Cisneros, Catherine of Genoa, and the Brothers and Sisters of the Common Life strove for their own and others' conversions despite entrenched corruption.

In the second stage of the Catholic Reformation from 1517 to 1545, the Protestant expansion seemed unstoppable. Millions of Catholics either left the Church or found themselves cut off from her due to the decisions of their political leaders. Europe was threatened by invasion by the Ottoman Turks during these years, a distraction to Catholic leaders. Those Catholics who remained in Protestant lands played defense, just trying to hold on to the faith. Some efforts like the Pilgrimage of Grace against Henry VIII in England failed. However, Catholic leaders in Fribourg, Switzerland, for example, moved quickly to escort undesirable preachers to the border and thereby preserved the faith there even though surrounded by many Protestants. Beneath the surface of these challenging decades, spiritual life stirred within the hearts of a new generation. Conversions took place that would have momentous consequences in later stages of the Catholic Reformation.

The third stage of the Catholic Reformation happened during the years of the Council of Trent (1545–1563). In response to the trauma of religious fragmentation, Catholic leaders finally addressed key doctrinal issues that had been challenged. They formulated an overall strategy of Catholic reform. They saw the problem was not doctrine per se but the need to express doctrine in fresh and clear terms. Their efforts did not bring reconciliation between Catholics and Protestants, and both sides largely gave up trying to dialog. They resolved on the Peace of Augsburg in 1555 that stipulated rulers would determine the religion of their territories. Meanwhile, the Jesuits began to fan out across Europe and the world.

The fourth stage of the Catholic Reformation (1563–1650) witnessed the implementation of the Council of Trent through the vigorous leadership of Charles Borromeo in Milan and other bishops, the continued global expansion of Catholicism, and the rise of Baroque culture. A certain maturity of reform was reached in 1622 when Pope Gregory V canonized Ignatius of Loyola, Philip Neri, Teresa of Ávila, and Francis Xavier in the new St. Peter's Basilica as the exemplars of the new age of Catholicism.

Up Close and Personal:
ST. TERESA OF ÁVILA

A mystic Carmelite nun, St. Teresa of Ávila felt called to reform her order according to its charisms to adhere more strictly to a life of contemplation and prayer. Her efforts caused many to criticize her and even to bring charges against her through the inquisitional courts (she was investigated but never brought to trial). By founding a new branch of Carmelites, she not only led a group of women to a deeper, more profound exercise of their vows but also bore the fruits of her contemplations in her writing. St. Teresa was named a Doctor of the Church in 1970, along with St. Catherine of Siena—the first two women to be declared doctors.

Born in 1515, this Spanish noblewoman discerned a call to the contemplative life with the Carmelites but grew disenchanted with the laxity she observed (and initially participated in too). The sisters were distracted by trivial and worldly matters, lured away from their true purpose and their focus on God. Teresa's solution was to form a new order of Discalced (or barefoot) Carmelites that focused on austere poverty and devout prayer. She traveled extensively, founding many religious houses or convents in Spain and inspiring holy men to do the same.

Teresa had a radical effect on the world in both her leadership and reform in the convent and in her writing. Her major works include her autobiography *Life of St. Teresa of Jesus*, *Interior Castle*, and *The Way of Perfection*, in addition to works of poetry and letters. Her teachings on mental prayer were based on her own experiences over time as she matured though her spiritual life. They can require caution when being approached, as is often the case with mystical writings, but contain a wealth of goods for the patient and diligent reader.

The Catholic Reformation exhibited respect for Church authority, emphasized those aspects of Catholicism (such as human free will and the saints) that Protestants denied, bolstered a distinct identity, reformed from the top down, emphasized integrating spirit and matter (as opposed to Protestants like Zwingli dividing them), and focused on the Church's universalism

over Protestant localism. Catholics held up their central religious authority and their global reach against Protestant fragmentation in a merely
European context as signs of the true Church

A Difficult Loyalty: The Catholic Reformation in Stage 2 (1517–1545)

As Protestant reforms gained momentum, Catholics suffered a lot, as seen
in the amazing story of one convent that struggled for existence in Germany. This was the cloister of St. Clare in Nuremberg. The journal of the
abbess, Barbara Pirckheimer (1467–1532), was discovered by an archivist
and published in 1852. The first English translation appeared in 2006. It
provides a window into the kinds of pressures Catholics felt to join the
Lutheran reform movement and how some of them negotiated to maintain their commitment to Catholic reform in the confusing decades before
the Council of Trent.

Barbara was born in Eichstätt, Germany, to a well-to-do and devout
family of humanist education. Seven of her eight sisters also entered convents. Taking the name "Caritas" when she joined the Poor Clares, she
became known as one of the most learned women of her time. Erasmus
likened her to Margaret More Roper, the highly educated daughter of
Thomas More in England. The great Renaissance artist Albrecht Dürer
dedicated his famous series of woodcuts on the life of the Virgin Mary
to her as a sign of his respect. Caritas led the girls' school and was unan-
imously elected abbess of St. Clare's convent in 1503, a position she held
until her death in 1532.

Catholic reform had already begun for St. Clare's in Nuremberg long
before Luther. The Colettine reform, a reform movement internal to the
Poor Clares led by St. Colette, rendered results by the mid-1400s. St. Clare's
convent deepened its devotion to inner renewal through pious exercises,
prayer, and frequent confession. The sisters there already considered

themselves a reformed convent by the time Luther's idea of reform arrived in their city.

An Independent City

Nuremberg was a wealthy, forward-looking community. Since the late 1400s, the city council had secured almost complete independence from outside authorities. It purchased from the pope the ability to govern the administration of the church separate from the local bishop. Luther's ideas began to percolate through the Augustinians in Nuremberg and through a circle of humanist elites gathering at the house of Willibald Pirckheimer, Caritas's brother. This influence pushed the city's spiritual autonomy even further. Caritas argued with her brother about the merits of Luther's ideas through their correspondence.

This set the stage for the city council's acceptance of Lutheran reform on March 14, 1524, after a public disputation. This decision ended Masses and feast days, destroyed relics, expelled the most vocal pro-Catholic voices, and mandated the conformity of the monasteries to the new faith. By the end of that year, the Augustinians had defected to Lutheranism. In May 1525, the Carmelites followed. The Benedictines all became Lutherans in July and the Carthusians in November. Only the Franciscans, the Poor Clares, and the Dominican nuns resisted the council's efforts to unify religious practice across the population.

The monks and nuns who left their religious lives discarded their habits and adopted secular clothing even while continuing to live in their religious houses, in many cases. Caritas noted, "A wild life ensued." In the name of Luther's "Christian freedom," no order was observed anymore, "with each person doing whatever he wanted to." Ex-monks ate meat during Lent. Some ran away and took wives. Many sold monastic valuables to provide income for themselves.[3]

Tremendous pressure from many different directions tried to compel Caritas and her sisters to capitulate to Lutheran reform. For example, in 1525 priests were forbidden to say mass for Caritas and her sisters. There was considerable unrest in the city, and unruly mobs surrounded the convent, cursing, shouting, smashing windows, and singing slanderous songs in the churchyard. Preachers thundered from the city pulpits that no convent should be tolerated any more. "We were very afraid and worried and could hardly sleep from fear," Caritas wrote.[4] People came to their relatives in the convent to warn them they were damned if they stayed. The nuns were compelled to listen to long Lutheran sermons. Caritas met with leading Lutheran theologians like Melanchthon, whom she respected, because he disagreed with the use of force against them. Still the Poor Clares would not yield.

Resistance and Respect

Caritas's journal begins with a letter to the city council appealing that the Franciscan friars be allowed to continue offering the sacraments to them. They had served the convent faithfully for nearly 250 years. This matter concerned the salvation of their souls. Caritas directed her letter to the superintendent Kaspar Nützel who represented them. "I beseech your honor humbly," she continued, "as if I lay at your feet, that you would protect your and my dear children from such a change."

Nützel had translated the *Ninety-Five Theses* and published them in Nuremberg. He was now an enthusiastic Lutheran and greatly desired the nuns to share in the new faith. Over the course of the journal, it is evident that Caritas and the superintendent grew to respect each other's differences. He called her "sister in Christ," and she addressed him as "prudent, wise, dear superintendent." On one occasion, she expressed her sorrow that as fellow Christians "your faith and ours cannot become the same." Because of such divergence, she desired they "practice moderation."[5]

Instead of the Franciscans, the council wanted to send Lutheran "lay priests," who were commonly ex-Catholic priests, to serve the nuns. Caritas was decidedly against this. She wrote to her brother-in-law, a high-ranking civic official: "It would be better and more useful to us if you sent an executioner into our cloister who would cut off all our heads rather than sending us fat, drunken, immoral priests." They could not confess to those who did not believe in Confession, or receive the Blessed Sacrament "from those who abuse it so disgustingly that it is upsetting to even hear about it," nor obey those "who are obedient to neither the Pope, the bishop, the Emperor nor the entire Holy Christian Church."[6]

She wrote to her brother-in-law: do not be moved by those arguing the word of God is concealed from us in the convent. "We have the Old and New Testament here within these walls just as you do outside these walls. We read it day and night in the choir, at table, in Latin and in German, in common and each on her own as she will." Against those who insisted the sisters were enslaved to human interpretations of the Bible, Caritas answered that if she were to accept any interpretations of the Bible, "then I will more certainly believe the interpretations of the dear, holy doctrine which are approved by the Holy Christian Church than interpretations of some alien mind which has been rejected and scorned and are preached by those who are, after all, merely human beings."[7]

Caritas gave much thought to the place of scripture in the reformation movements around her. She noted how "everyone uses the scriptures for his own purpose and no one will give in to another and there is no end in sight." So many "highly educated people" opposed each other, even among the "evangelicals" [Protestants] themselves. There were errors all about. Some were denying Christ's divinity while others got rebaptized. Karlstadt, Zwingli, and Luther—all considered themselves true prophets. "Now everyone wants to force the other person to believe and do what he wants," Caritas wrote. She admitted there were many abuses in the Church, but her convent had already accepted Catholic reform. If they simply accepted everything that is called "God's Word" by the reformers around them, "then we would, perhaps, fall from one sect into another, as has happened to some people." Therefore, she wrote cunningly, according to the claims of "Christian freedom" propounded by Luther himself, they would not allow themselves to be forced into the new teachings.[8]

Negotiating Catholic Reform

The threat of forced reform and the actual use of force against the nuns is evidenced throughout the journal. "These people [the Protestant reformers]," she wrote, "did everything with great force." But Caritas refused to use force herself. She resolved not to hold back any sister who wanted to leave. Only one out of about fifty did so. But just as she would force no one in the convent to remain a Catholic nun, she would not accept force applied to herself or any of her nuns to be Lutheran.[9]

Early in 1525, Ursula Tetzel, the mother of one of the Poor Clare nuns named Margaret, came to see Caritas at the convent. She demanded entrance in order to speak privately with her daughter about a matter affecting her salvation. Caritas replied it was not possible to open the convent in such a way. Margaret herself implored Caritas not to open the door. She was afraid her mother would drag her out of the convent by force and that she would not be able to defend herself if the door was opened. After Ursula left, Margaret ran to Caritas and the other sisters sobbing. She pleaded with them not to let her be torn away from her community and her vows.[10]

Ursula appealed to the city council. She said she and her husband had given up their daughter Margaret to the convent as a "living sacrifice" for her salvation in the old days of religious darkness. "Now, however," she wrote, "I have learned so much from listening and reading that I believe that the cloistered life is unknown to God and is nothing but a human invention, a heretical deviation." She insisted, "My conscience has forced me along with my two brothers to demand that the honorable abbess [Caritas] give my daughter back to us." She asked the council for help arranging for her daughter to be transferred home so she could listen to the Word of God. Margaret would then be free to remain or return to the convent.[11]

The nuns also appealed to the council: "The plaintiff does not have the power to take her daughter from the cloister against her will. Her daughter is not obligated to follow her either against her conscience." Margaret's mother was making a false appeal to conscience. She had done her duty in giving a warning to her daughter. Margaret now bore the responsibility of decision, not her mother. Caritas closed by offering a biblical defense of their cloistered life. "We want to follow the example of the first Christians of whom it is written in the Acts of the Apostles that they were all together and shared everything in common, both possessions and money. . . . They went to the temple daily and praised God. This was a true cloistered life too."[12]

Frustrated at the impasse, superintendent Nützel met with Caritas in private and urged her to convert to the "proper path." That would "do him and the entire City Council the greatest of favors, for they liked me very much and were well inclined toward me. If they only had me on their side, then they would have the entire community." The leaders of the men's religious communities had all conformed. Only Caritas was "headstrong" and "disobedient" toward the councilors.[13]

When Nützel was through speaking, Caritas wrote, "I took courage." She told him she was overwhelmed at how ardently he was concerned for their souls, "since by virtue of your office the care of our souls is not your responsibility. You are only the guardian of our temporal goods. Thus you have assumed a power which you do not have. . . . You desire of me that I should direct the sisters to do things that are against my conscience. That I will not do out of fear or favor of anyone."

In this time of confusion when "no one really knows what to believe," Caritas told Nützel, "we have all decided to remain in the old faith and in the clerical state and do not want to accept anything which has not been accepted by the Christian Church." Her sisters had strictly forbidden her to accept anything at all, and even if she told them to convert, they would not. The sisters understood clearly their proper autonomy within the city.

They would never give up the abbey's freedom of election. "No one has the right to interfere."

"In this way we argued with each other for a long time," Caritas wrote. Nützel "believed we should trust the City Council in everything. I felt no." She pitied him for being led astray by false teachers. She told him, "In the times of Arius and other heretics things proceeded the same way when people were misled with sweet-sounding words." He disagreed. "More grace is raining down than in a hundred years," he said. "Each believed the other was blind and mistaken."[14]

"Here I Stand"

The most dramatic section of Caritas's journal recounts the events of June 13, 1525. They concerned Sister Margaret Tetzel (age twenty-three), the young nun already mentioned, as well as Sister Katharina Ebner (age twenty) and Sister Clara Nützel, daughter of the superintendent (age nineteen). On this day, their mothers arrived with men to remove them from the convent. All three young women fell to the floor, screaming and crying. They wanted to hide, but Caritas would not let them, concerned if they did the crowd would break in and search the whole convent, making everything worse. The entire convent wept.

Caritas led the young women into the chapel, the exclusive space for the cloistered nuns to participate at Mass while separated from the rest of the congregation. The "fierce she-wolves," as Caritas called the mothers, entered the church with the men. They drove out all the people and locked the church door. Caritas opened the convent door separating the chapel from the church, presumably under orders from the council. She did not hold back anyone inside the convent by force. The mothers wanted Caritas to step through the door into the church, symbolically leaving the convent with the young women. Caritas refused. The older women wanted her to force the young nuns to go out into the church alone. She refused this too, leaving the decision up to the young women. "None of them would cross the threshold in any way," Caritas wrote. To the young women, the threshold between the private chapel and the public church represented the boundary they had embraced in their vows and was the basis of their identities.

The mothers then asked the men to "finish things up," for they were afraid of a riot. Caritas spoke to the men, telling them to go into the chapel and talk with the women so they would cooperate. "I could not and would not force them to do what was repugnant to them from the depths of their hearts," Caritas wrote. Two men entered the chapel. Caritas and the other sisters withdrew and locked the door so no one could enter the convent proper.

The mothers rushed into the chapel and ordered their children to leave. "The brave knights of Christ defended themselves by word and deed as much as they could," Caritas wrote, listening from the other side of the chapel door. The young nuns wept and pleaded.[15]

The mothers insisted their daughters obey them, citing the fourth commandment—"Honor your father and your mother" (Ex 20:12). If they remained, they were in the jaws of hell. In good conscience, they could not allow their daughters to stay.

"You are the mother of my body, but not of my spirit," Katharina Ebner said to her mother, "for you did not give me my soul. For that reason I owe you no obedience in matters which my soul opposes." Her mother insisted she herself bore responsibility before God. The three mothers argued with their daughters, threatening them in all manner of ways. Katharina spoke very courageously and supported her statements with the words of holy scripture. She tried to convince the mothers that in using force they acted contrary to the Gospel. She spoke so eloquently for an entire hour that afterward the men said they had never heard anything like it.[16]

Neither side would give way to the other. The mothers threatened to tie their daughters' hands and feet and drag them out. The nuns would not yield.

At this point, Caritas came back into the chapel. She wrote, "There stood my poor little orphans among the vicious wolves and defied them with all their strength." She greeted the mothers and told them she had brought their children here as the city council had ordered. Now they saw their will in the matter. The mothers demanded Caritas release them from their vows. The abbess said she had no authority to do so, but she could release them from their obligations to her authority. The mothers seemed content with that. The young women declared together they did not want to be freed from their vows. "We want to keep what we vowed to God," they said. They appealed to Caritas, but the abbess said, "Dear Children, you see that unfortunately I cannot help you, for the forces here are too great. You would not like to see even more misfortune befall the convent."

Katharina Ebner responded, "Here I stand and will not yield," words that echoed—ironically!—those of Martin Luther at the Diet of Worms in 1521. "No one shall be able to force me out," she continued. "If I am removed by force, however, it shall never be by my will in eternity."[17]

At that moment, one of the men took Katharina and dragged her out of the chapel. Caritas and the other sisters fled. They heard the quarreling, shouting, and fighting among the screaming, weeping young women. They were now technically out of the convent and in the church. The mothers tore the habits off their daughters and put worldly clothes on them.

Just before the nuns were placed in the waiting coaches, they appealed to the people gathered. They were suffering abuse and injustice. Katharina's mother punched her in the mouth to make her shut up. Nearby soldiers said they would have helped the young women if they had not feared a riot. Hundreds ran after the vehicles as they pulled away.

"What happened afterward to the poor children among the vicious wolves," Caritas wrote, "we cannot know." She heard Clara did not eat for four days and the others cried unceasingly. The city council demanded the convent continue supporting the young women financially, presumably until suitable husbands could be found for them. Left without any other options in that age, all three nuns eventually married. They always spoke highly of the convent.[18]

Despite these personal tragedies, Caritas's expert negotiation—constantly informed by the opinions of the other sisters—managed to preserve the existence of the convent. The nuns believed grace would help them live the vows they had made. This sustained them in their decades of spiritual isolation, deprived of Mass, Confession, and last rites. After Caritas's death in 1532, her sister and then their niece governed as abbess. When the latter died in 1563, the city took over the convent and used it as a home for aged nuns. The city council allowed the convent to continue, but they forbade any new members. This led to its eventual demise.

Tragedy in an Ecclesiastical State

Shortly after Caritas died in 1532 while the Poor Clares struggled to hold on in Nuremberg, a tragedy unfolded in northwest Germany. It shocked all of Europe. It also led to the first major Catholic success against Protestant expansion. This event was the Münster Rebellion of 1534–1535.

The whole region was divided into small ecclesiastical states governed by prince-bishops with both temporal and ecclesiastical power. They were largely secular lords who exacted heavy taxes on the laity and paid vast sums to Rome every time they were elected to their positions by the aristocratic canons (governing priests) of the cathedrals.

Like Nuremberg, the city of Münster had gained increasing autonomy from its bishops and outside political authorities. It was virtually a "city church" even before the arrival of radical reform ideas. This spiritual isolation made it vulnerable.

The canons of the cathedral who elected the prince-bishop lived the lives of noblemen, though they gave alms too. One staunch Catholic historian alive at the time, Hermann von Kerssenbrock, remembered before the rebellion there was an admirable "connection of friendship and closeness between clergy and laity." Laymen treated the clergy, including monastics, with much deference in both public and private. "The laymen treat them with such honor and reverence that you would think them not mortals but gods on earth."[19] This sort of clericalism made Luther's opposite "priesthood of all believers" idea attractive to some.

Wealth exacerbated the social disparity. The clergy did not have to pay taxes and could claim tithes. Monasteries entered into economic competition with guilds without having the civic burdens the laymen had to shoulder. In Kerssenbrock's view, wealth led the clergy to be negligent and to meddle in others' affairs. The laity grew ambitious, defiant, and envious of other peoples' property. Then Satan "waylaid the prying, mutinous hearts of men," Kerssenbrock wrote. "Through the clever use of these hearts he first introduced dissension and disagreement about the worship of God." Lutheran ideas took hold. A huge conflict between clergy and common people arose as "each man strove not only to defend his own view tenaciously but also to propagate it as far as possible." Anticlericalism bubbled beneath the surface and fueled social revolution. The resulting misfortune was of an "incredible magnitude."[20]

On January 13, 1534, the self-proclaimed Anabaptist prophet John of Leiden passed unhindered through the city gates of Münster. He had potent ideas and emotions—conviction of divine inspiration, hatred of idolatry and moral corruption, and apocalyptic belief that the day of the Lord's vengeance was at hand.

This sense of apocalyptic urgency was felt by many people at this time due to a general sense of crisis. There was the internal crisis of religious division in Europe and an external crisis of foreign invasion. The (Muslim) Ottoman Turks had conquered much of the Christian Kingdom of Hungary in 1526 and attacked Vienna in 1529. They seemed poised to invade Germany next. Surely the final judgment was imminent.

In this context, John of Leiden and his companions preached in the streets of Münster. They looked up to the heavens, groaned, and screamed out the need for repentance. Many listened intently. But to those who taunted them, the prophets said, "Woe, woe, woe to you! Woe, woe to you, who make fun of those who are driven by the spirit of God, who do not accept the healthy word 'repentance.' . . . Repent! Come to your senses! Do not call down upon yourselves the vengeance of the Heavenly Father!"[21] Other prophets arrived to reinforce this message.

Taking advantage of political indecision and an atmosphere of "freedom of conscience," the prophets and their allies took control of Münster City Council one month later. They expelled Catholics and Lutherans who would not join their cause. They destroyed religious art across the city, burned all books except the Bible, instituted communal ownership of property, mandated polygamy, and replaced the municipal government with a "council of elders"—all in the name of the Word of God. They thought the established system was so corrupt that violent cleansing was justified. Better to annihilate and start over. John of Leiden was eventually crowned king of the "New Jerusalem" (Münster). He was recognized as the all-powerful leader of the battle against the Antichrist in the last days.

In response, the Catholic prince-bishop Franz von Waldeck besieged the city with both Lutheran and Catholic troops. He believed he was dealing with revolutionaries. He warned the Catholic powers of Europe that they meant to destroy governments everywhere and conquer the world. Waldeck managed to secure aid from other princes across the region and from the wider Holy Roman Empire. As their encircling trenches cut off supplies, John of Leiden and his henchmen enforced their regime through terror, spiritual manipulation, and execution of dissenters.

Waldeck's forces eventually conquered the city in June 1535. John of Leiden was tortured to death. His mangled body was put in a cage and hung from a church steeple. A replica still hangs there today, a testimony to the dangers of spiritually isolated reforming zeal and bad religion.

Combatting Bad Religion

Corrupt religion encourages followers to violate natural law. It sparks terrorist acts today just as it did back in the sixteenth century. The Münster Rebellion inspired other upheavals like an attempt by radicals to take over the city of Amsterdam. This shocked Europe and led to hundreds of executions. Rulers put in place tighter regulations on the printing industry in some areas. After these events, Anabaptists pivoted away from apocalyptic reform toward strict pacifism and ethical principles under the leadership of the ex-Catholic priest Menno Simons.

Private revelation and biblical interpretation cut off from the wider Christian community led to disaster. There are remarkable parallels between the Münster radicals and Islamic terrorists today. The latter take Koranic interpretation into their own hands. Indoctrinators suppress conscience while making their followers *think* of themselves as devout. Such radicals infiltrate societies using "freedom of conscience" to end freedom of conscience. And they oppress women—just like the reformation radicals in Münster. Bad religion is a human problem, not just a Christian or an Islamic problem, and Catholics confronted it vigorously in the sixteenth century.

The Rest of the Story

Prince-bishop Franz von Waldeck lived in concubinage and was sympathetic to the Lutherans. However, his retaking of Münster was the first and most dramatic event of the second stage of the Catholic Reformation to counter aggressive Protestant expansion. Even as England, Denmark, and Norway all followed Protestant ideas of reform in the 1530s, parts of northwest Germany remained nominally Catholic. It was not until the pope began appointing some cathedral canons and the Jesuits started arriving in the 1580s that re-Catholicization really took place. But the military victory at Münster laid the groundwork.

Ignatius of Loyola

As rogue prophets infiltrated Münster in 1534 fueling apocalypticism, compulsion, and religious violence, a remarkable group of friends formed at the University of Paris with a much different religious mentality. They believed God's creation was fundamentally good. To experience true freedom, human beings must use God's creation wisely to attain him. Driven by their conviction that seeking God's glory above all things redounds to one's own happiness, this band of brothers (including university students and young professors) conceived of a common mission. They did not think of starting a religious order but envisioned meeting the widely felt needs of their time in a new way. That excited them.

Up Close and Personal:
ST. IGNATIUS

St. Ignatius of Loyola lived a life of intensity in all things. A soldier seeking glory before his conversion, he persuaded his commanding officer at the Battle of Pamplona to try to hold out against the siege of the French on their garrison, despite the opposition of the governor. In this battle, he was struck by a cannon ball and wounded severely in both legs. Despite the pain he endured in his convalescence (with no anesthesia), he asked to have his leg rebroken and set correctly later.

His passion was better served after his conversion, when his operating principle became *Ad Majorem Dei Gloriam* or "to the greater glory of God." Ignatius's drive to do better—to do more—was relentless, but now it had a proper end. After his conversion, he spent three days confessing his sins, trying to cover his whole life. Even after this confession, he spent nearly a year consumed with extreme scruples about his past. It took radical trust in God, exercised over time, for him to find peace again. It was out of these experiences his Spiritual Exercises began to form.

He threw himself into spiritual practices, imitating the great saints he had read about during his recovery. He fasted, begged, prayed for seven hours a day, made pilgrimages, and sought spiritual masters to help him. God blessed him with mystical experiences, allowing him to receive immense truths as if he were a student sitting in the classroom.

After his ordination, Ignatius would cry profusely as he said Mass, sometimes fearing he would be unable to complete his priestly duties. He worried his eyesight would give out because he spent so much time in tears. He was also a prolific letter writer, some sources saying he wrote more than 6,800 letters for the members of his order, as a spiritual director, and for other ministerial and administrative duties. Under his care, the Jesuits grew to more than a thousand members before his death.

At their center was Ignatius of Loyola, a soldier from northern Spain. Recovering from battle wounds, he had read *The Life of Christ* by a theologian known as Ludolph the Carthusian that had been translated into Castilian through one of the translation projects of the Spanish reformer Cardinal Cisneros. After years of prayer, service to the poor, and study, Ignatius developed a robust training program in holiness, a thirty-day retreat called the Spiritual Exercises. Its very name countered the "faith alone" theology of Protestant reform. Ignatius tapped deep into Catholic tradition—and his own experience—to emphasize the possibility of human cooperation with God's grace. God alone saves man, but man with the help of grace can respond heroically. Human effort can unlock more grace, sparking a kind of feedback loop of growth in holiness. Ignatius's sanctity was forged in suffering and it was immensely compassionate and attractive. Ignatius's friends passed through the exercises in 1534. Each man independently resolved to follow Ignatius wherever God might lead. Despite their great differences, the whole company made but "one man," without constraint in their association. They made all decisions by majority vote, but they were always unanimous.[22]

At sunrise on the Feast of the Assumption of Mary, 1534, Ignatius and his friends passed through the city walls of Paris to the rustic hill of Montmartre just outside. There was a little chapel on the side of that hill where they congregated. Peter Favre, the only priest among them, said Mass. They all pronounced a vow of chastity and poverty. They resolved to go to the Holy Land or, failing that, Rome to offer their services to the pope for the salvation of souls. After Mass they picnicked on the hill and made merry, celebrating the great day. They did not know it, but they had just made history.[23] Out of their actions that morning sprang the Society of Jesus, and its members—called "Jesuits"—would span the recently circumnavigated globe within decades.

Ignatius's Idea of Reform

As Ignatius matured during the 1520s and 1530s, many people around him pushed different reform agendas. There were pseudo-mystics in Spain and Paris who believed personal union with God made external worship, sacraments, and concern for sin irrelevant. There were the Lutherans who held to *sola scriptura* and other Protestant groups who tried to eliminate spiritual mediation through the Eucharist, sacraments, and sacred art. There were certain disgruntled Catholics and humanists like Erasmus who were critical of the Church and often wrote in sarcastic or ambiguous ways.

Ignatius took a different approach. He never adopted the belief that everything was doomed or that it was his responsibility to "reform the Church." He was intent on helping souls, beginning with his own. For him, the Church was a mother and a divinely established institution—William

Langland's "woman with the beautiful face." It embodied the kingdom of Christ. In response to its many defects, Ignatius employed quiet, positive, and constructive tactics. As one theologian wrote, these tactics "aimed chiefly at interior reform of individuals" through conversations and the Spiritual Exercises.[24] This approach to reform proved so fruitful the Jesuit order grew out of it. The Jesuits formed the first organized educational system in the world open to anyone. They launched missions on several continents. They conducted an effective response to Protestantism that brought many back into the Church.

Influenced by his early love of chivalry and knighthood, the key word of Ignatian reform was *loyalty*. He wrote "Rules for Thinking with the Church" at the end of his Spiritual Exercises. The intention was for the retreatants to first fall in love with Christ and the idea of serving him and his Church: "With all judgment of our own put aside, we ought to keep our minds disposed and ready to be obedient in everything to the true Spouse of Christ our Lord, which is our Holy Mother the hierarchical Church."

Other rules specifically countered Protestant influence. Ignatius counseled retreatants to praise marriage—but religious vows even higher. They should venerate relics and ask the saints for intercessory prayers. "We should extol . . . pilgrimages, indulgences for jubilees and crusades, and the lighting of candles in churches," he wrote. One should take care that in highly praising *faith* one did not "give the people an occasion to grow listless and lazy in their works." He thought emphasizing divine grace should not "generate a poison harmful to freedom of the will." Ignatius did not tell people how to think about these challenging questions. Rather, he gave practical advice for living with questions and continuing to ponder them. Thinking with the Church meant also thinking for oneself. This mature "both/and" approach to doctrine and rational autonomy, faith and works, and God's grace and human effort was at the heart of Jesuit spirituality and reform.[25]

Clarifying Identity: The Catholic Reformation in Stage 3 (1545–1563)

Many people longed for a council to address Luther's claims and to resolve the confusion of the time, but it was twenty-eight years after the *Ninety-Five Theses* before one met. Why so long?

There were two main reasons. Popes feared a council would try to trump papal authority as the one at Constance (1414–1418) had attempted to do. In addition, regular warfare between King Francis I of France and Holy Roman Emperor Charles V from 1521 to 1544 made it nearly impossible to hold a council in the empire—where both German Catholics and Lutherans insisted one take place.

At last, peace made it possible to convoke a council at Trent in northern Italy. At that time, Trent was technically part of the Holy Roman Empire and close enough to Rome to ensure regular communication with the pope by currier. It was a compromise location.

Despite fathering four children as a cardinal and engaging in nepotism, Pope Paul III (r. 1534–1549) is remembered as the first pope committed to reform. In the bull he issued convoking the Council of Trent in 1545, he lamented the hatreds, dissensions, and heresies of the age. The Ottomans, who threatened Germany from their base in Hungary, had also landed troops in southern Italy in 1537. There was fear of a general invasion. To make matters worse, Christian kingdoms constantly fought each other, and the "affairs of Christendom . . . became worse day by day," Paul III lamented. Everyone was "overwhelmed with apprehension and grief." There was understandably an immediate need for a council to heal the confessional split, reform the Church, and establish peace for the sake of common defense against the Ottomans. The pope wrote that "we have resolved to trust in the clemency and mercy of God rather than distrust our own weakness, for in undertaking good works it often happens that where human counsels fail the divine power succeeds."[26]

The council needed regular injections of divine help. There were disagreements about priorities: Charles V, the emperor, wanted the council to focus on reforms, but the pope wanted it to simply clarify doctrine. While the council fathers were determined to deal with both concerns alternately, an epidemic of typhus ended the first period of the council with much work left incomplete. The second period lasted from 1551 to 1552. Lutheran theologians presented their case, but the Catholics realized there was no hope of reconciliation. War in the empire ended the second period with little accomplished. The next pope opposed resuming the council, so ten years passed. Finally, the rise of Calvinism in France was such a threat to Catholicism there that it seemed only a council could help the situation. This prompted the third and final period of the Council of Trent from 1562 to 1563.

Decisions of the Council of Trent

"The holy Council of Trent, lawfully assembled in the Holy Ghost," declared the Second Session of the Council in 1546, "has ordained and decreed that each and all of the faithful of Christ assembled in the city of Trent be exhorted . . . to amend themselves in the evils and sins hitherto committed and to walk henceforth in the fear of the Lord."[27] Personal reform needed to precede any discussion of reform of the Church.

By the fourth session (1546), the council took up leading Protestant claims. The council fathers felt no need to address issues that few people at the time questioned, such as the Trinity. Rather, they moved right into the question of justification, or the transformation of a sinner into a holy son or daughter of God. This was the heart of the matter in the Age of Reformations. Addressing central Protestant concerns, the council fathers asserted that people are damaged by original sin and that they are saved by God's grace alone. The Fall of humanity, however, did not put humans totally at odds with God, as many of the Protestant reformers held. Rather, human beings retained their free will and ability to cooperate in their salvation. Good works are gifts of God and at the same time merit an increase of grace and glory within the justified. Human beings can participate in God's glory. "You have wrought for us all our works," Isaiah wrote (26:12). Man and God work together on the lifelong project of salvation.

The council also discussed the scriptures. In opposition to the Protestant principle of *sola scriptura*, the council perceived that the Gospel of Jesus Christ was contained "in the written books" and in "the unwritten traditions" received by the apostles from Christ and handed down to later generations. The council reaffirmed the traditional canon of scripture and addressed the problem of interpretation. In order to check "unbridled spirits," the council decreed that "no one relying on his own judgment shall, in matters of faith and morals pertaining to the edification of Christian doctrine . . . presume to interpret [the scriptures] contrary to that sense which holy mother Church . . . has held and holds." The one doing so distorted the scriptures "in accordance with his own conceptions."[28] Poor Clare abbess Caritas Pirckheimer had made the same argument in her Nuremberg journal, and the devastating events at Münster proved the danger of ignoring it. Interestingly, the council did not address the nature of the Church or the papacy. There was too much divergence even among Catholics for that. Clarity on those matters came only hundreds of years later with Vatican Council I and Vatican Council II.

The Council of Trent also dealt with pastoral concerns. Bishops had to attend to their flocks in their dioceses. They needed to establish seminaries for the education of priests. The meanings of indulgences, relics, and images were all clarified and defended.

YOU BE THE JUDGE:

Did the Church sell forgiveness of sins?

No, the Church has never sold the forgiveness of sins. The buying and selling of spiritual things is a mortal sin called simony (see Acts 8:9–24). The Church has never taught that forgiveness, which is freely given by God, can be purchased.

This misunderstanding comes from the Church's practice of granting indulgences. An indulgence is not the forgiveness of sins. It is the remission of temporal punishment incurred by sin. What does this mean? When one sins, there are a couple of results. First, there is damage to one's relationship with God—mortal sin cuts off relationship; venial sin weakens it. But a second result occurs too: the person who sins is *wounded by the sin*. This can mean a lot of things—it may be more difficult to avoid the sin later because a habit or disposition is created, or an attachment to a worldly good or to the sin itself might be formed, and so on. These wounds need to be healed, even *after* the sin is forgiven in the sacrament of Confession. This is where indulgences come in—they are pious acts aiming to counter and heal the *wounds* of sin. Temporal punishment refers to the temporary, but real effects that sin has on a person. These effects must be dealt with in this life or in purgatory.

Indulgences grew out of the severe penances that used to be attached to the sacrament of Confession in the Early Church. Eventually penances lessened from lifelong requirements or things like multiple years of fasting every third day to less severe ones that could be completed before the penitent died. By the sixth century, the Celtic Church had codified them into simpler, prescribed penances based on monastic influence. This would go on to influence the rest of the Church as well. Things like pilgrimages, alms to support churches, and other charitable works for the church—such as building hospitals, orphanages, and so on—became associated with indulgences too.

The theological understanding of indulgences developed over time. They are available to the Church militant (those on earth) and can be applied to the Church penitent or suffering (those in purgatory) because they are all part of the Mystical Body of Christ written about by St. Paul in several of his letters. Christ's sacrifice stored up infinite merits in heaven that can be applied through the authority of the Church to the members of this mystical union. The saints add to this treasury too, though it is understood that Christ's sacrifice was all that was ever needed. Christ as the head vicariously satisfied the debts of his members.

Indulgences were misunderstood because they were misrepresented by various churchmen who did not make the theology behind them clear. Instead, they made them sound like a one-way ticket to heaven for purchase to bypass purgatory. This is not, nor has it ever been, the case. In fact, the Church had already condemned these abuses in the Fourth Lateran Council (1215).

The council members grew exhausted by the end of 1563 as they tried to finish by the deadline imposed by high costs of the meeting (18 percent of the annual papal budget). When the great moment came to close the council, two hundred bishops gathered in the cathedral to praise God for the end of an important chapter in Church history. One of the legal advisers keeping a diary recorded the moment: "I cannot possibly communicate what joy all present felt, and how they blessed God. . . . I saw so many grave and distinguished prelates, with tears of happiness flowing from their eyes, congratulating even those with whom they earlier were at odds."[29] The Council of Trent laid the basis for modern Catholicism until Vatican Council II.

Implementing the Council

Trent's original hope of reconciliation with the Protestants stalled. The council changed direction from seeking common ground to emphasizing differences. Naturally, due to its papal sponsorship, Protestants utterly rejected it. Yet even some Catholics did too—just as after Vatican II. The Venetian priest Paolo Sarpi published his *History of the Council of Trent* in 1619 in London to avoid censorship. He questioned papal authority over any council of bishops. He argued the Council of Trent had failed to enact true reform because it was manipulated by the popes. The Tridentine church was just a tool of Roman administrators.

Other Catholics disagreed on how to interpret the council's document on justification. On one hand, Luther proclaimed "faith alone" and denied the role of free will and good works in salvation. On the other, secular-minded Renaissance thinkers glorified in unassisted human effort. The council took a middle position. God's grace is the basis of human salvation. But human free will can respond, or not, to grace. Responding positively to grace disposes a person to receive more grace. Good works are the result of both God's grace and human effort. As St. Teresa of Ávila put it in her *Autobiography*, we must beg God for virtue, for "if we exert our own efforts, He will deny to none."[30]

A major dispute broke out between Dominicans and Jesuits about how to reconcile divine grace with human freedom. The Dominicans thought the Jesuits emphasized free will too much, and the Jesuits thought the Dominicans did not emphasize it enough. Eventually, Church authorities would have to forbid any further argument between them due to increasing rancor. This same controversy exploded later in the seventeenth century between the Jesuits and the Jansenists—a strict Catholic movement condemned by the papacy in 1653 and 1713. As one historian wrote, these disputes showed the "limitations of the written word, especially when it touches on matters of deep personal concern."[31]

In addition to dissent and to passionate debates about conciliar inter-pretation, a certain "spirit of Trent" shaped how the council was under-stood afterward. The council itself refused to create a theological system out of respect for freedom of multiple interpretations and the limits of theological formulation. However, in opposition to Protestant and later rationalist arguments, some postconciliar Catholics interpreted Trent as a complete theological system. They misinterpreted faith as rigid unifor-mity, tended toward biblical literalism, and promoted papal monarchism. The "spirit of Trent" (the way it was interpreted by some people), similar to the "spirit of Vatican II" in our own era, contributed to serious errors in prudential judgment as in the Galileo affair.

Nevertheless, Trent unleashed tremendous energies toward the renewal of Church and culture. Piety, mysticism, and theology were reborn. The art and culture of the Baroque age exploded across the Cath-olic world, reaching beyond Europe from Peru to India. One historian noted the Tridentine reform was the first truly global initiative in history.[32]

A New Age of Culture: The Catholic Reformation in Stage 4 (1563–1650)

Pope Pius IV (r. 1559–1565) moved immediately to put the papacy at the head of Catholic reform as the Council of Trent ended in 1563. He confirmed and promulgated the council's decrees. This eased the strains between reform-minded leaders and the papacy that had disturbed Chris-tendom for two hundred years in debates over conciliarism. Thankfully, after Pius IV died, the reforming flame passed to Pope Pius V (r. 1566–1572). He is currently the only pope recognized as a saint between Celes-tine V who resigned in 1294 and Pius X who died in 1914.

Up Close and Personal:

POPE ST. PIUS V

It is difficult to look at the Age of Reformations without feeling the acute lack of holy leadership during the time. The Church is comprised of sinners as well as saints, and it is true that not every pope who has worked as an administrator for her has always offered the best of themselves. This makes Pope St. Pius V stand out even more clearly as a bulwark of Catholic Reformation efforts that followed the Council of Trent. His papacy lasted from 1566 to 1572, and in this short time he accomplished a lot to build up Catholicism from within by instituting the council's decrees.

Coming from a life of poverty working as a shepherd, he joined the Dominicans around 1518 at the age of fourteen. After his ordination to the priesthood, he was eventually installed as a bishop and appointed an inquisitor general for many years before being elected to the papacy in 1566. Right away, Pius's decision to continue to wear his Dominican habit set the tenor of his papacy, allegedly inspiring the tradition of the pope's white cassock worn to this day. He practiced other ascetical disciplines, continuing austerities he had previously adopted. He also continued to work with the poor, caring for them in person and with funds typically reserved for some of the opulence of the papal court.

The Council of Trent had finished a few years before, and Pius wasted no time in instituting its reforms. His short reign as pontiff included the completion of the Catechism of the Council of Trent, which was used until Vatican II. It had been suggested by Charles Borromeo, and its aim was to educate the clergy, though it was available for the laity as well. He also revised the Roman missal and breviary (thus standardizing the Roman rite for the Mass), supported the Jesuits in their missionary work, and declared St. Thomas Aquinas a Doctor of the Church. He organized the Holy League to answer the threat of the Ottoman Turks whose conquest through Europe was ever advancing. This led directly to the victory of the naval battle of Lepanto. During the battle, Pius asked that churches remain open and the faithful pray the rosary to ask the Virgin Mary's intercession. When he heard of the victory, he declared October 7 to be a feast in honor of Our Lady.

His papacy was not without controversy and difficult decisions. After years of seeing the persecution and disenfranchisement of Catholics in England under the reign of Elizabeth I, he issued a papal bull in 1570 excommunicating her. This resulted in even more severe treatment of the Catholics there: it effectively nullified her as their leader, and she sought revenge for this. It became very dangerous to be a Catholic in England, deadly, in fact. Pius sought to support the members of his church in one of the only ways available to him, hoping to embolden them to stand up to their oppressive ruler. Many died as martyrs for their faith.

The saintly pope was assisted in his reforming efforts by another saint: Charles Borromeo (1538–1584), who had worked with papal representatives to bring Trent to a successful conclusion. Having passed through Ignatius's Spiritual Exercises, Borromeo traveled from Rome to Milan to become the first archbishop to reside in the see in more than eighty years. The place was a mess. Many priests dressed in secular clothes, carried weapons in public, and lived in open concubinage. Much of the clergy was relatively uneducated. There was a common saying at the time: "If you want to go to hell, become a priest."[33] Many convents hosted balls and festivals. One group of Benedictine nuns prostituted themselves. Much of the laity had ceased going to the sacraments and knew little of the faith.

Up Close and Personal:

ST. CHARLES BORROMEO

Charles Borromeo was born into wealth, power, and decadence in 1538. He could have lived a life of comfort typical of clerics of the Renaissance Church, but instead his parents taught him to genuinely love Christ and his Church. Borromeo lived a life of virtue, even as a young and privileged man. He surrounded himself with holy and talented people, befriending other future saints like Philip Neri, Aloysius Gonzaga, and Edmund Campion.

His unique administrative gifts served the Church well in its response to the Protestant Reformations sweeping through Europe. As a cardinal and archbishop, he was an antidote to the corruption witnessed in the clergy prior to the reforms: a steady, conscientious reformer who saw his position of power as a responsibility and an opportunity for service, not one for selfish aims. He was a powerful force behind the implementation of the Council of Trent.

Interestingly, Borromeo's pastoral sanctity and devotion to reform would greatly influence a later council: Vatican II. Pope John XXIII, who called Vatican II (1962–1965), was a historian who spent his early career editing a critical five-volume edition of documents from Borromeo he had discovered in an archive in Milan. The texts described Borromeo's visitation to the diocese of Bergamo in 1575 in the wake of Trent. They revealed how involved he was in the life of each diocese near Milan, and how he sorted through problems ranging from financial woes to improper clerical behavior and an insufficient number of Masses. In his studies, John XXIII realized the Council of Trent had not just focused on countering the Protestants and defining doctrine. It was also about pastoral renewal, concern for souls, and the reform of church disciplines. John XXIII believed this was exactly what the Church of the mid-twentieth century needed, and Borromeo gave an excellent example of how to accomplish it. His studies of Borromeo and Trent provided a historical framework by which he could enunciate his vision of the Second Vatican Council. We must learn from history, John XXIII said in his opening address at the council in 1962, which is the "teacher of life."[34]

Then Borromeo arrived. He resolved to implement the council, and many sensed their comfortable lifestyle was about to change. Some tried to kill him, including two friars while Borromeo was praying vespers in a church.

Nevertheless, Borromeo worked tirelessly. He reorganized diocesan administration and called provincial councils and diocesan synods to coordinate reform. He also opened a seminary and established the Collegio Borromeo, which still exists to support worthy and needy students at the University of Pavia south of Milan. He approved a Jesuit college and organized hospitals as well as shelters for abused and abandoned women and children. He promoted the Confraternity of Christian Doctrine for teaching the catechism to children. When the plague struck, he gave away his own clothes to the poor and organized spiritual and physical support for the sick and the dying. No wonder many came to love and admire him.

In 1577, he wrote a booklet for laypeople on living the faith in "every state in life," especially for fathers and mothers of families, masters of workshops, and workers. In it he wrote a prayer: "Bestow [a new heart] upon us, Lord, with such abundance of your grace that it will produce in us, efficaciously and constantly, new resolutions, new customs, a new way of life and in the end that eternal renewal . . . Jesus Christ . . . came into the world to bring us."[35] This prayer was a seed of the new Catholic culture taking shape by the power of the Holy Spirit, to whom Borromeo was much devoted.

The reform work that Borromeo and his clergy accomplished was recorded in the *Acts of the Church of Milan*. This book circulated widely in Europe in many editions. When Borromeo was canonized in 1610, it gained even more traction because it showed what a diocese reformed according to Trent looked like. His model of reform would inspire the wider Catholic world.

Borromeo also published a book of detailed instructions on church architecture and furnishings. He preferred classical and functional principles. He required confessionals to be installed in the body of the church. These structures were known before Borromeo's time, but his influence led to near universal usage among Catholics. He imagined a reformed church architecture in his diocese that would cultivate a calm and dignified ambiance for prayer. The book was distributed among priests, architects, and builders. It contained detailed directions for everything from altars to choir stalls. The influence of Borromeo on church architecture spread across Europe and beyond to Mexico, New Orleans, and Quebec.

Adaptable Jesuits

If Borromeo exhibited a new episcopal ideal, the Jesuits were a new kind of religious order never seen before. Pope Paul III had approved their establishment in 1540. The founding constitution defined the basic mission. Whoever wanted to be a "soldier of God" resolved to serve the Lord alone and his vicar on earth, the pope, in mission work. Members would "strive especially for the progress of souls in Christian life and doctrine." They would labor "for the propagation of the faith by the ministry of the word, by spiritual exercises and works of charity, and specifically by the education of children and unlettered persons in Christianity."[36] There was no mention of countering Protestantism. Jesuit renewal developed from an independent movement of evangelical energy that would only later directly counter Protestant influence.

The Jesuits would be mobile like Franciscan and Dominican mendicant orders, but they would bring an entirely new and shocking way of Christian life into the world. Ignatius and his original group of friends did not conceive of themselves as "traditionalist" reformers trying to shore up the old religion. They believed change was the best means of preserving the Catholic faith. Jesuits vowed poverty, chastity, and obedience, but they did not wear any fixed habits as did members of religious orders. They also did not ask members to pray together at set times or practice strict bodily discipline. "We are not monks!" one of Ignatius's close collaborators, Jérôme Nadal, constantly repeated to the others.[37] These arrangements allowed them maximum flexibility in their work in the world.

This must be understood against the background of Ignatius's experience in Manresa, Spain. From 1522 to 1523, while Luther's and Zwingli's ideas spread rapidly in Germany and Switzerland, Ignatius spent long hours in prayer and practiced severe fasting and other austerities. But he also exercised an early form of his "discernment of spirits" by paying attention to what was happening inside him in the midst of his asceticism. He consulted his inner experience—as Luther did—but in dialog with the Church. Ever since his initial conversion he had noticed that certain reflections gave him more peace than others. He took this as an indication of God's will. Ignatius noticed at Manresa that when he lessened the severity of his penances, his serenity of mind returned. He found himself more able to help others. As one historian wrote, Ignatius turned away from "the model of sanctity that prevailed up to that time, which assumed that the more severely the body was punished, the better the soul would flourish. It assumed that the greater the withdrawal from 'the world,' the holier one would be." By contrast, Ignatius turned back *to* the world as a result of his experience at Manresa. He later insisted that Jesuits take proper care of their physical health in the service of God. He did not prescribe set penances. They should make full use of natural goods, particularly when interacting with others. "Not monastic silence was the ideal," one historian wrote, "but cultivation of the art of conversation." Jesuits accepted whole heartedly the admonition of Thomas Aquinas that grace builds on nature. This was a significant moment in the history of Catholic spirituality.[38]

It met considerable opposition. Many Catholics did not understand the Jesuits, whose untraditional lives aroused suspicion and whose phenomenal success caused bitter rivalry. The Faculty of Theology at the University of Paris, considered the most prestigious in the world, published a decree in 1554: "This Society [the Jesuits] appears to be a danger to the Faith, a disturber of the peace of the church, destructive of monastic life, and destined to cause havoc rather than edification." The prominent Dominican theologian Melchior Cano said the Jesuits were part of a sectarian movement with heretical leanings as dangerous as Lutherans or Calvinists. Others characterized Ignatius's Spiritual Exercises as a kind of mysticism in which God's direct communication with the soul undermined the sacraments and other practices of the Church. Ignatius continually defended the orthodoxy of his Spiritual Exercises before the Inquisition. Criticism did not stop even when his book was published with papal approval.[39]

The Jesuit Idea of Reform

The Jesuits did not set out to "reform the Church" or defeat Protestantism. Their idea of reform was indirect. They were to

- start with themselves—make use of the Spiritual Exercises;
- minister to laypeople or individual monasteries through preaching missions, spiritual directing, and serving the needy and sick;
- encourage frequent communion and Confession; and
- found schools.

They hoped helping people to holiness would spread reform among wider and wider circles. The Jesuit ministry set a new pastoral standard.

The Ministry of Education

Establishing schools had not been part of Ignatius's original vision. Managing schools would work against the mobility he had prioritized for the order. However, Ignatius consented to one school in Sicily in 1548. Requests soon arrived for more schools. Ignatius quickly realized their importance and how they might contribute to the wider Jesuit mission and to influencing the culture. "All the well-being of Christianity and of the whole world depends on the proper education of youth," one prominent Jesuit said a few years after the school in Sicily opened.[40]

By the late 1560s, Jesuits ran about 150 schools. By 1606 that number jumped to 293. Jesuit schools appeared not only in Europe but also in Latin America, India, and Japan. By creating the first free public education system spanning the globe, Jesuits blazed a path for later Catholic educational endeavors that have profoundly shaped the mission of modern Catholicism.

Jesuit schools aimed to educate laypeople—not clerics—for "worldly" careers as civic leaders and entrepreneurs. No religious order had systematically pursued such a goal before. The Jesuits adopted the most advanced educational principles of the day found in Renaissance humanism and wedded them to formation in Christian doctrine. The Jesuit historian John O'Malley noted that humanistic pedagogy, derived from classical antiquity, was radically student centered. Its goal was to produce *good men* dedicated to the common good of both Church and state. This meant forming the whole person for both civic life and Christian life, ideally woven together into one life.[41]

Boys from ages nine to eighteen studied grammar, rhetoric, Latin, Greek, mathematics, science, literature, and history. Jesuit priests or Jesuits in training taught the pagan classics of ancient Greece and Rome—not just the usual theology and philosophy. The Jesuits tried to lay the groundwork for an integration of faith and reason in the lives of students. "To search for truth, goodness, and beauty in any subject was to search for God, and to magnify God's glory."[42]

The study of literature included drama, which meant that some Jesuits wrote and staged plays, unheard of for a religious order. Theater "taught poise," O'Malley wrote, "and put eloquence, the mark of a leader in society, into practice." Playacting sparked enthusiasm in students.[43] In addition, it often entailed music and dance. The Jesuit Collège Louis-le-Grand in Paris became so famous for its dance performances that the French king and aristocracy would attend. This created a scandal of worldliness in the eyes of other Catholics who opposed the Jesuits and their methods.

Because the Jesuits believed grace builds on nature, they excelled not only in theology and philosophy but also in humanistic and scientific fields. For example, the German Jesuit Christopher Clavius (1538–1612) became probably the most respected astronomer in Europe. He helped establish the Gregorian calendar in 1582, named for its sponsor, Pope Gregory XIII. This is the most widely used calendar in the world today. Due to their worldly interests, Jesuits "developed a profile that, in comparison with other orders, looked decidedly secular," O'Malley wrote.[44] Again, this brought them a lot of criticism throughout their existence until today.

Incredibly, Jesuit schools were free. The inscription at the entrance to the Jesuit school in Rome (1551) read, "School of Grammar, Humanities, and Christian Doctrine, Free." They financed such institutions in different ways, as Ignatius once laid out in a 1551 letter to a fellow Jesuit. A city, ruler, private individual, or group of people would "furnish an annual sum of money."[45] This required massive efforts toward fundraising, wherein Ignatius excelled. The principles of Ignatian fundraising included:

- valuing work (Ignatius admired business entrepreneurs and their single-mindedness);
- letting one's light shine through newsletters, publications, and letters in order to show others the value of the work being done;

- knowing one's donors and being patient with their moral failings;
- practicing good stewardship of resources; and
- honoring one's friends and supporters and showing gratitude to them.[46]

With a sound financial basis in place, Jesuit schools opened their doors to anyone. At one school in Billom, France, for example, 7 percent of the students came from the nobility, 33 percent from the business and political class, and the rest from the lower classes. This openness brought different kinds of people into close contact with each other, refining them and forming wide swaths of the culture through education.

Jesuit schools played an important role in the Catholic Reformation. They became respected civic institutions and provided vocations to the Jesuit order who could then create additional ministries. They also proved an effective means of countering Protestantism. Jesuits opened their schools to everyone, regardless of religious background. "The allure of a free top-notch education proved irresistible to many non-Catholic parents," one historian wrote, "and the result was the conversion to Catholicism of many entire families, even of whole regions."[47] For example, by 1560 Polish nobles steadily converted to Calvinism. It looked as if the entire country would move in that direction. With royal support, however, the Jesuits established schools—twenty-eight of them by 1626. These helped preserve Catholicism in the country. Good preaching helped too. Listening to Jesuit sermons became fashionable, even for Protestants. All of this helped Poland return to its traditional Catholicism.

The work of the Jesuit Peter Canisius (1521–1597) produced similar effects in German-speaking lands. Born in the Netherlands, Canisius attended the University of Cologne. There he heard about the new religious order called the Society of Jesus. In 1541, he made the Spiritual Exercises under the direction of Jesuit Peter Faber (1506–1546), who had cofounded the order with Ignatius and their original circle of friends.

Canisius decided to join. He attended the Council of Trent as a theological advisor and then went to Germany to teach theology at the University of Ingolstadt. Later in Augsburg he revived the stagnant Catholic community there with his preaching. He played an important role in founding schools in the southern half of Germany, in Austria, and in Switzerland. The schools produced many leaders of Catholic reform later in the 1500s. The effects of the schools were denounced by Protestants. Against the school at Mainz, for example, one Protestant wrote, "The progress of the Holy Gospel was greatly hindered there by the Jesuits, men whom the devil has hatched out in these latter times as his final brood for the corruption and ruin of the Church of God."[48]

Canisius also wrote the first series of Catholic catechisms that countered Luther's catechisms in a serious way. They remained in use for four centuries and appeared in hundreds of editions in many languages. He was a leading force of the Catholic Reformation and was designated a Doctor of the Church in 1925.

The Catholic Reformation and Baroque Culture

The Catholic reform movement of the 1500s advanced spiritual ideals, theological norms, and ecclesiastical structures that became prominent in Catholicism for more than three hundred years. It also inspired a new form of culture now called "Baroque." Baroque culture endured well into the 1700s across Europe, into Russia and India in the east, and throughout Spanish and Portuguese America in the west. It influenced many of the arts from architecture to drama and music. In painting, it employed movement, exuberant detail, and appeal to the senses to instill surprise and awe. Baroque culture arose from multiple influences, including humanism and the often-passionate and even sensual language of Catholic mysticism.

The Council of Trent gave impetus to this Baroque culture in two ways. First, in the theology of the decrees on original sin and on justification, the council fathers affirmed traditional Catholic teaching that human nature is not inherently sinful even if it is inclined to sin. Through baptism, human beings become entirely new creations. They are called to put all their spiritual, intellectual, and physical faculties to good use in order to realize the highest goal of creation: the glory of God. The council defended such Christian humanism against the pessimism of Luther and other Protestant reformers about human nature. While justification proceeds from the predisposing grace of God through Jesus Christ, human beings may "convert themselves to their own justification by freely assenting to and cooperating with" grace, the council said. It continued: when the scriptures say, "Return to me, says the LORD of hosts, and I will return to you" (Zec 1:3), people are reminded of their liberty. When they respond, "Restore us to yourself, O LORD, that we may be restored!" (Lam 5:21), they confess the need for the grace of God.[49] This Christian humanism reflected the cooperation of human beings with God and fed directly into Baroque culture

Second, the Council of Trent spoke directly about the arts in its twenty-fifth session in 1563. It proclaimed the importance of retaining images of Jesus, Mary, and the saints in churches in response to the widespread iconoclasm of the age. This reaffirmed Catholic tradition, building on the Second Council of Nicaea's affirmation of image veneration in AD 787. By means of these images believers could adore Christ and honor the saints. Paintings instruct and confirm people in the faith. Images should inspire people to "fashion their own life and conduct in imitation of the saints and be moved to adore and love God and cultivate piety."[50] Bishops should guard against superstition surrounding images and against anything unbecoming, confusing, or seductive.

This Tridentine theological approach acted to rehabilitate the senses and bodily activity in worship, ritual, and the arts. In response to the Platonic spiritualism of the Renaissance and the separation of spirit from matter by Protestant reformers, incarnational Baroque culture joined body and soul together in tense harmony and explosive creativity.

This integration worked toward the redemption of the body and of the whole person. One spiritual writer described how the Spanish mystic St. John of the Cross (1542–1591) referred to the senses as the "lower part" of the soul. They are meant to be the main way human beings experience God's goodness. Each of the five senses can help lead one's soul to rest in God. *Sight* beholds the goodness of God's creation. Believers are called to see other people as God sees them. *Hearing* is called to take in the Word of God so we can obey it. *Touch* is meant to be pure and to help us love and serve each other. *Smell* reminds people of the sweetness of little sacrifices offered to God and the stench of sin. *Taste* is a pleasure that draws us to the nutrition we need, both physically and spiritually. Purifying the senses through asceticism (self-denial) draws spirituality and physical vitality *together*. The "higher part" of the soul included intellect, memory, and will. Purifying these through faith, hope, and charity—along with physical asceticism—restored human beings to the fullness of life to which Christ called his followers.[51] The revival of Aquinas and of scholasticism in the late 1500s also worked to preserve this unity of body and spirit within human persons and support the creative explosion of Baroque culture.

Baroque Architecture and Painting

Against an avalanche of Protestant writings undermining the sacraments, Baroque architecture and painting supported a uniquely Catholic response. They attempted to influence viewers at a deeper level than just intellectual argument, in mystery conveyed through the senses. For example, the Church of the Gesù was the first new ecclesiastical structure built in Rome after the Council of Trent. It was inspired by Charles Borromeo's writings on ecclesiastical architecture and served as the mother church of the Jesuits. Begun in 1568, the stunningly beautiful Gesù unambiguously demonstrated the centrality of the Eucharist to anyone who entered its doors. Everything in it directed one's attention toward the altar and tabernacle. A communion rail replaced the traditional rood screen, gathering people instead of separating them from the sacred. Art historian Elizabeth Lev noted that this church building reinforced the message of Ignatius's Spiritual Exercises, which welcomed one's senses to participate in prayer through imaginative meditation. "The Gesù invited the laity to taste, touch, see, hear, and smell the presence of the Lord."[52] This countered Zwingli's view when he wrote that "whatever binds the senses diminishes the spirit." While earlier Catholic reformers such as Erasmus would have had some sympathy for his position, Baroque culture utterly repudiated it. Here, in the Church of the Gesù, the senses worked to magnify the spirit.

In addition to the Sacrament of the Eucharist, Baroque painting portrayed repentance and Confession. The great painter Titian (ca. 1488–1576) had won fame and wealth with his sensual paintings of mythological scenes. However, he attended one of the sessions on penance at the Council of Trent later in life after his wife, daughter, and grandchild had all died. From then on, he produced fewer secular scenes and focused on Jesus Christ. A late painting now attributed to him is *Christ and the Good Thief* (ca. 1566). The good thief on his cross turns to Jesus to confess his guilt. The composition is arranged as if it were in a confessional. Jesus is painted turning to the side listening with head bowed, so as not to shame the penitent. In Lev's interpretation, "the daring perspective not only isolates the two figures in the powerful moment of redemption, but Jesus' outflung arm invites us, too, to share our sins with Him, to shoulder our penance and bask in the warmth of His mercy."[53]

Other paintings reaffirmed the importance of the Virgin Mary and her intercession in contrast with Protestant rejection of mediation between Christ and believers. Caravaggio's *Madonna of the Rosary* (1607) is a good example. The composition places the Virgin Mary seated above a crowd directing St. Dominic to distribute rosaries to all the people gathered. Mary hears everyone's prayers. At the same time, baby Jesus stands on his mother's lap at the very center of the work. Caravaggio conveyed here that people can go straight to Jesus. But the Virgin Mary's role is to help them do so. The *Madonna of the Rosary* was probably commissioned to celebrate Marcantonio Colonna's victorious command of the papal fleet at the 1571 Battle of Lepanto defeating the Ottoman Turks.

Catholic Baroque painting proclaimed that Christ continues to touch us physically. This countered the Protestant ideas common at the time that miracles ceased after the time of the apostles and that only "spiritual" practices help us closer to God (things like listening to sermons). Catholic mystics and artists believed that just as Christ in his body encountered the people around him and healed them during his lifetime on earth, so he continues to encounter us physically in our own time. God can reach us through the material world—most commonly in the Eucharist but also through relics, holy places, and holy people.

For some, this physical encounter with Christ was so intense it reportedly left physical marks. The artist Federico Barocci (ca. 1535–1612) created the painting *St. Francis* around 1600. Barocci had a personal devotion to St. Francis and pictured him in a cave praying before a crucifix and the Bible. Francis gazed intensely and loving at Christ with glistening eyes, "shining with inner energy," Lev wrote. Francis has just received the stigmata, or the wounds of Christ, on his hands, feet, and side. "The passion of the saint's prayer has evoked an experience from the Word of God to the presence of God."[54] From the perspective of Baroque culture, this empirical reality of God-is-with-us served as an ultimate witness to the true physical presence of Jesus in the Catholic Church.

The Catholic idea of reform through the senses directly countered the Protestant tendency to relegate encounter with God to the intellectual, spiritualized sphere. "Catholic art strove to manifest the experiential, even the sensual, nature of oneness with the Lord," Lev wrote. It also challenged viewers to think of their own lives in Christ as works of art, she added. People can participate in their salvation by responding to unearned grace, shaping their way of life through purification of the senses and through faith, hope, and charity as a unique artistic interpretation of the life of Christ. This created a beautiful gallery of holiness in the lives of the saints.[55]

Baroque Rome

After the papal corruption of the early 1500s and the sack of Rome by the mutinous troops of Emperor Charles V in 1527, a newly energized city finally started to take shape late in the century. The popes planned for transformation. They wanted to engage pilgrims, tourists, and diplomats with astounding beauty, appealing to their minds through their hearts. They reorganized piazzas, roads, and churches to welcome pilgrims, direct them to sacred sites, and propose an idea of reform in continuity with the whole history of the Church. For example, laborers accidentally rediscovered the Roman catacombs in 1578. They found graves ornamented with Christian paintings, Greek and Latin inscriptions, and carved sarcophagi. This created a sensation. For the first time, people realized an entire city lay beneath their streets. It was like discovering another world, one connecting Catholics visibly back to the early Church. This seemed to prove Catholic continuity over Protestant novelty.

In addition, beautiful fountains slaked the thirst of pilgrims visiting the city of Rome and reminded them of the cleansing waters of baptism. The 1651 Fountain of the Four Rivers was designed by the talented architect Bernini for the Piazza Navona in Rome. It represented the four major rivers of the four continents through which Catholicism had spread around the globe: the Nile in Africa, the Danube in Europe, the Ganges in Asia, and the Río de la Plata in South America.

At the time, missionary work appeared an unmitigated success story. Some sensitive people recognized even then certain abuses were happening against native populations. Yet, missionary work, even when imperfectly implemented, affected the Catholic idea of reform in two ways. First, it made Catholicism the first global religion. This seemed to prove the authenticity and universality of the Church as against Protestant claims. It showed Catholics had been faithful to Christ's command to "go therefore and make disciples of all nations" (Mt 28:19). Second, the global missions helped Europeans start to think of their own lands as mission territories. Various areas of their home countries were also full of people in need conversion—and not just among Protestants. Rural and mountainous areas contained many unevangelized European "natives."

The greatest event amplifying the new role of Rome as the center of global Catholicism occurred in 1622. In that year, Pope Gregory XV (r. 1621–1623) inaugurated the Congregation for the Propagation of the Faith to coordinate missionary activities. In addition, St. Peter's Basilica was nearly complete. Its construction had partly caused the Protestant Reformations through the abuse of indulgences, but now it became the site of four triumphant canonizations: St. Philip Neri, Ignatius of Loyola, Francis Xavier, and Teresa of Ávila. These were four champions of the Catholic Reformation who had helped to put the faith back on the firm foundation of holiness. The walls of St. Peter's were decorated with red hangings and tapestries. A vast crowd filled the nave. Trumpets blared and applause echoed. There was a solemn liturgy with Sistine Chapel singers. In addition, local ceremonies in Spain, the homeland of three of the saints, mirrored events in Rome, underscoring the bond between local churches and the papacy strengthened by the Catholic Reformation. Since two of the saints were Jesuits, the order held additional celebrations at the Jesuit Roman College over several days. Students danced, sang, and performed elaborate theatrical events. The year 1622 marked a high point in the Catholic Reformation.

Chapter 4

Consequences

The Complex Legacy

From the Catholic point of view, the Council of Trent was the greatest legacy of the Age of Reformations. It deeply influenced Catholic culture. So did the profound mystics, energetic Jesuits, and talented artists of the time. There was a higher concentration of Doctors of the Church in the 1500s than in any other century except for the 300s.[1] The legacies of these great figures in doctrinal clarity, artistic beauty, and commitment to education continue to nourish people today.

On the other hand, the Age of Reformations introduced complex and troubling problems. The most obvious of these was fragmentation of Christianity in Europe and beyond. In 2017, Catholics and Lutherans drafted a document that lamented this result: "We must confess openly that we have been guilty before Christ of damaging the unity of the church."[2] Christ prayed "that they may all be one; even as you, Father, are in me, and I in you, that they also may be in us" (Jn 17:21), and the Christians of the sixteenth century let him down.

But this was not the first time Christians broke unity. Different Christian traditions (not in communion with Rome) developed out of the debates in the fifth and sixth centuries over the relationship between Jesus Christ's human and divine natures. These included the Church of the East in upper Mesopotamia and the Oriental Orthodox churches in Africa and the Middle East. Communion between Rome and the Eastern Orthodox Church in Europe and Russia ended in 1054 for theological and political reasons. These happened before the sixteenth century.

There was something different about the Age of Reformations, how-ever. The division seemed endless. Protestant groups diverged from each other as much as from Catholics. The printing press meant that *sola scriptura* made sense to many people because books became widespread. This new situation seemed to give unprecedented ability to individuals to interpret divine revelation on fundamental doctrine for themselves. The growth of state power and the strengthening of national identities further undermined religious unity.

Scholars have interpreted the global significance of these religious fractures in different ways. The sociologist Rodney Stark, for example, claimed that modern Christianity is better off despite all the splitting—or even *because* of it. He wrote the Age of Reformations did not "secular-ize" the world because religion today "is stronger than ever worldwide." Indeed, the Age of Reformations brought about more good than harm, Stark thought, particularly for Catholics.

Stark thought pluralism (multiple Christian denominations) is what makes Christianity the fastest-growing religion in the world today, because it results in "more active and effective churches." They must compete for members and influence, and that competition keeps them fit. Stark wrote, "The Catholic Church actually thrives on Protestant competition and is far more successful and effective when forced to confront it."[3]

It is true that Protestant competition spurred Catholics to greater catechetical labors by the late 1500s. Nevertheless, in contrast to Stark's argument, historians have pointed to negative outcomes of pluralism. As independent churches worked to counter each other's influence, they often adopted anxious, defensive, and controlling attitudes. The "inquisitorial principle" gained momentum in the Age of Reformations from London to Geneva and Rome.[4] Nuance in biblical interpretation dropped out, and Catholic leaders made major blunders against freedom of religion in France in the Revocation of the Edict of Nantes (1685) and against proper boundaries between religion and science in the Galileo affair (1616–1633).

A narrow authoritarianism created a dangerous breach between the Church and the wider culture that has born bitter fruit in our own time.

Thus, several historians have argued, religious division contributed to *secularization*, or the retreat of religion's direct cultural influence. It was during the religious fighting from 1550–1650 that "the ground was prepared for the secularization of European culture," Christopher Dawson wrote. Brad Gregory claimed that *sola scriptura* "created an unintended jungle of incompatible truth claims among those who rejected the Roman church." These incompatible convictions unintentionally led to a secular society, ironically, even though all the reformers set out specifically to make their societies *more* religious. Similarly, Carlos M. N. Eire noted that religious fragmentation created spaces for secular forces to flow. The militant struggle for orthodoxy strengthened churches, but it also generated rancor between them. This process generated skepticism, even atheism, and was "a most significant step in the de-Christianization of Europe."[5]

While it is not immediately clear how to reconcile these different theological, sociological, and historical views of religious unity and fragmentation, it is possible to examine more deeply certain positive and negative consequences of the Age of Reformations.

The Paradigm Shift

Christian religious sensibilities today have changed dramatically since the 1500s. For example, the Second Vatican Council addressed themes like the central place of vernacular translations of holy scripture in the life of the Church and the priesthood of all believers. It also examined the need for continual reform in the Church, the understanding of church offices as service oriented, and the importance of freedom in human relations—particularly religious freedom. Interestingly, these were many of the concerns Protestant reformers expressed in the sixteenth century. If Catholics had clearly emphasized these truths at the time of Luther, would the Protestant

Reformations have even happened? But would these changes have happened within modern Catholicism *without* the Protestant Reformations? It is hard to say, but certainly developments within Christian culture during the Age of Reformations forced Catholics to clarify their faith and develop their understanding of it, both as taught and lived.

These religious developments since the 1500s represented a change in worldview so deep it realigned much of subsequent thinking. This paradigm shift had practical implications for the way faith was lived. The Age of Reformations represented a major shift from "medieval" to "modern" sensibilities.

Risking overgeneralization, medieval sensibilities involved "sacralization," and the Age of Reformations inaugurated "desacralization." Sacralization meant associating particular people, things, ceremonies, and places to the sacred or to the spiritual—something common in the Middle Ages. Priests, relics, exorcisms, and pilgrimage sites operated as portals of influence between the physical and the spiritual worlds. Sacralization also linked political rulers, talismans, spells, natural forces, magical healing, and many forms of superstition to spiritual power. For good and for ill, this was all common in the Middle Ages.

Desacralization, on the other hand, meant loosening these links between worldly things and the sacred. This happened in certain sectors of the Renaissance and Protestant Reformations. The forces of nature were just natural. Priests were just regular people. Bones were just bones. Bread was just bread. Pilgrimage sites were no different than any other. Desacralization was not the same thing as secularization or loss of faith, but rather it redrew spiritual boundaries from within the Christian community. Desacralization was "a process of subtraction from within, of Christians eagerly reducing the scope of the supernatural on earth, rather than a process of erosion by external factors of any kind."[6] Many Protestants denied the Sacrament of the Eucharist, prayers for souls in purgatory, and postbiblical miracles. While all of creation comes from God, desacralization separated heaven from earth.

Catholics reacted against desacralization in the Catholic Reformation by preserving and adapting strong connections between heaven and earth. The Catholic Reformation, especially in its Baroque form, tried to *re*-sacralize the world. It attempted to link it again more tightly to the divine in response to Protestant sensibilities. Catholics held that human beings mingled the spiritual and the material because they are a soul animating a body. Humans lived in the presence of unseen but powerful spiritual beings, such as angels and demons, who affect their lives. Catholics supported this worldview by emphasizing the real presence of Jesus Christ in the Eucharist and by blending the natural and the supernatural in their art and in their piety.

However, Catholics came to accept a greater desacralization in their religion and in their lives as a kind of refinement due to the Reformations. They eventually de-emphasized relics, created tighter guidelines for recognizing miracles in the canonization process, and cracked down on superstitious piety. Eventually, clergy were no longer seen as "gods on earth" as they were in Münster before the Anabaptist rebellion. They were desacralized to some degree, as were political leaders. This process of better distinguishing between the natural and the supernatural was jump-started by humanist scholars and the Protestants and gained traction among Catholics during the Catholic Enlightenment of the eighteenth century and during Vatican Council II in the twentieth.[7] This all happened even as Catholics emphasized more than ever frequent reception of Holy Communion and Confession. Thus, Catholic culture adapted to certain "modern" sensibilities as it has always adapted to new historical conditions.

The history of Christian culture from the Age of Reformations to today has produced give-and-take between periods of desacralization and other periods of sacralization. Both impulses on their own contained dangers. Desacralization alone could lead to extreme privatization of religion, loss of the sacraments, and a purely secular public sphere. Sacralization, on the other hand, could lead to theocracy, loss of personal religious freedom, and lack of respect for the proper autonomy of the natural order. One needed to check the other. The tensions between them create much of the historical dynamic of Christian culture.

Aligning Church and State

In two areas, however, the Protestant Reformations did *not* immediately work toward desacralization during the Age of Reformations. One was belief in the devil's influence on daily life through magic and witches. Luther constantly complained in his writings about being tormented by devils. In the "witch craze" between the 1560s and the 1680s, both Catholic and Protestant populations executed up to sixty thousand people accused of some form of witchcraft which was seen as a public crime.

Historians do not clearly understand why this witch craze happened. But it overlapped with the second area in which desacralization did not occur: the relationship between Church and state. Among both Protestants and Catholics, states increasingly sought to control churches and their societies in the name of "reform." Perhaps the human tendency to demonize enemies converged with the desire to purge society of evil through political power, resulting in the witch craze. Regardless, politics and religion more and more aligned in the Age of Reformations, expanding on tendencies already present in the late Middle Ages.

Churches were often eager to cooperate. In fact, they relied on state power to promote their rival theological views and for protection against their enemies. The medieval Catholic Church, due to historical contingencies and fidelity to the words of Jesus (Mt 22:21), did not align completely with any state as the later Lutheran Church in Germany or the Church of England did in the Age of Reformations.

By the 1500s, however, Catholics increasingly subjected the Church to state control. Secular rulers took reform and global missionary work into their own hands. King Ferdinand and Queen Isabella obtained a large amount of power over the Catholic Church in Spain. Pope Pius IV complained that their great-grandson King Philip II "meant to be pope as well as king."[8] Independent German cities like Nuremberg or Münster secured virtual domination over the Church within the bounds of their jurisdiction well before 1517. All through the later 1600s, Catholic France worked to deepen the church-state alliance within its borders, persecuting the Protestant minority. Political rulers became religious authorities.

While most Catholics and Protestants worked to harness their churches to their states, the Radical Protestants moved in a different direction. After their failed experiment at Münster, Anabaptists and other Radicals decided to completely detach from politics. They made certain accommodations to state authorities in order to live as peacefully and separately as possible. Alternatively, they migrated out of the reach of European states to the North American colonies. Their descendants, such as the Amish, the Mennonites, and the Baptists, contributed to the eventual desacralization of politics and the separation of church and state as it emerged in the eighteenth century.

Catholics found this modern situation amenable to eventually reestablishing themselves in the English-speaking world. Many Catholics now conceive of the state as primarily concerned with temporal goods, not spiritual ones. They have seen how the privatization of religion after the Age of Reformations can lead to new forms of public intervention and religious witness.

Confessionalization

Greater state control of churches during the Age of Reformations corresponded with a process historians call "confessionalization." This refers

to the formation of churches with well-defined identities, precise con-
fessions of faith, and rigorous codes of ethics.[9] People started to think of
themselves as "Catholic" or "Lutheran" and understand their identities
in contradistinction to each other. Caritas Pirckheimer, the Poor Clare
abbess, showed more of the older way of thinking when she wrote of the
"Holy Christian Church," not the "Catholic Church," even as her negotia-
tions with Lutheran authorities in Nuremberg strengthened her Catholic
loyalties in the 1520s. She did not think in terms of "churches" but of simply the "Christian Church." This changed throughout the 1500s toward
vigorous denominational identities.

Confessionalization led to a greater concern for patrolling the boundaries of orthodoxy, or "correct belief," and moral practice. The attempt
to enforce belief and behavior did not always work very well. Ten years
into his reformation in Germany, Luther lamented, "The peasants learn
nothing, know nothing, do nothing but abuse their liberty. They do not
pray, confess, or take communion, as if they had been freed from religion
altogether. As they once used to ignore popery, they now turn us away
with contempt."[10] This situation revealed starkly the gap between ideals
and lived realities that gave urgency to reform. Reforming zeal appeared
to justify strengthening the link between churches and states. This made
social control—for the sake of the common good—seem both desirable
and possible. The Genevan Consistory was organized in 1541 to integrate
church and political life by enforcing morality and Reformed beliefs in
Geneva. Among Catholics in the Italian peninsula, the Roman Inquisition
started in 1542 to combat Protestant influence. Rome started banning the
reading of Protestant books in 1559.

Protestant states and churches in particular cooperated in coercing
people to practice religion. For example, in England the state compelled
attendance at Anglican services on penalty of fines. German Lutheran
princes mandated church attendance, the taking of Communion, and
baptizing infants. In Lutheran Sweden, soldiers appeared on the streets on

Sunday to make sure everyone was at church. In Norway and Denmark, one could not be a citizen without being a Lutheran. One was fined for not attending church services. Churches were wielded as tools for state purposes—often with their enthusiastic collaboration. People believed coercive efforts such as these would help close the gap between Christian ideals and social realities. Religious confessionalization set a precedent for modern attempts to enforce ideological alignment of people, even in secular contexts. Reform by force would leave a troubling legacy.

Convergence of Religion and Violence

One of these troubling legacies was a convergence of religion, politics, and violence from the earliest years of the Reformations until the Thirty Years' War (1618–1648) and the English Civil War (1642–1651). These two conflicts alone caused the deaths of up to seven million soldiers and civilians. Some have tried to argue that this violence was not caused so much by "religion" as by politics and other concerns.[11] While there is merit to this point of view, historical research has shown much of the violence that occurred in the Age of Reformations can be linked to religious differences. Besides wars, this violence took the form of iconoclasm (the destruction of religious images), rebellions, persecutions, and massacres. For example, some Protestants desecrated Catholic churches, images, and consecrated hosts across Europe in trying to rid communities of "idolatry." (Some Catholics practiced iconoclasm too, especially outside Europe when conquering the Incas and the Aztecs.)

Another kind of violence was rebellion and attempted revolution. Both the German Peasants' Revolt of 1524–1525 and the Münster rebellion in 1534–1535 were examples. Preachers proclaimed the need to kill the ungodly before the end of the world came. The rhetoric of violence used by the leaders of these movements rejected compromise and defended their idea of Bible-based reform to the death. Civil powers—both Catholic and Protestant—violently crushed such movements.

Then there was the violence of persecution that produced martyrs. This first happened in 1523 when a Catholic inquisition court tried two Augustinian monks for publicly professing Lutheran doctrine. The men refused to recant and were burned at the stake in Brussels by political authorities. Such people were viewed as martyrs by their fellow Protestant believers and celebrated in pamphlets, books, songs, paintings, and engravings. Some five thousand men and women, both Protestants and Catholics, refused to renounce their faith and were executed during the Age of Reformations as martyrs.

At the time, both Catholic and Protestant leaders felt they had sound reasons to persecute and fight each other. They held that heretics deserved a painful and public death as a warning to the rest of the community if they refused to convert. Christian magistrates believed they had a duty to defend God's honor, the common good, and true religion. Concerned about the threat to social disorder and acting on historical precedent, rulers prioritized the corporate over the individual, the soul over the body, and eternal life over earthly life. There seemed to be a "duty" of intolerance. In fact, tolerance was undesirable to most of the people of this age because many preferred to live in a world in which truth did battle.[12] For example, even as he worked for peace, Doctor of the Church St. Lawrence of Brindisi (1559–1619) directly influenced the militarization of Catholicism in Germany by helping to inspire the Catholic League in response to the Protestant Union of 1608. St. Lawrence was a biblical scholar, a missionary, and a warrior who believed any form of compromise with an enemy is wrong. People with different ideas of reform battled each other.

Militarized religious ideologies could lead to decades of fighting and even massacres, as in France where the Catholic majority held to the principle "one king, one law, one faith." Public rituals in France at the time, such as religious processions, usually involved *both* Church and political leaders. The unity of the body politic was reinforced, for example, by eucharistic processions of the Body of Christ. As the Reformed Church spread widely in France—there were more than two thousand churches by 1561—tension and then civil war emerged. How could two faiths operate in the same geographical space? Protestants attacked Catholic churches, which they believed promoted false worship. Catholics were horrified by sacrilege and fought back. Tragically, once the fighting started, no one could stop it. There were sieges, assassinations, and executions in France for more than thirty years. This led to angry publications, and these texts fueled the next wave of violence.

A low point in the French "Wars of Religion" was the St. Bartholomew's Day Massacre in 1572. The French king came to believe that the Protestants were plotting to assassinate him. Following his order, soldiers killed a few of the Protestant leaders gathered in Paris for a wedding. Seeing this, mobs of Catholic Parisians then began wildly hunting down their Protestant neighbors. They killed two or three thousand people in their homes or out in the streets and dumped their bodies into the Seine River. As news radiated out from Paris, thousands more Protestants met their death across the country. It seems many Catholic leaders around Europe believed a Protestant conspiracy existed in France. Since it was "thwarted" by the killings, many expressed relief at the news—even Pope Gregory XIII in Rome. In reality, however, this tragedy only led to decades of additional revenge and violence.

The poisoned legacy of bloody conflict during the Age of Reformations endured into the early twenty-first century as a touchstone for secular arguments against religion. The sins of Christians during the Age of Reformations "provided a firm launching pad for ideological and institutional secularization" in the modern world, one historian wrote. This happened because their sins created a "reservoir of resentment" and memorably associated religion with coercion, oppression, and violence. This seemingly provided evidence that emancipation, autonomy, and modernity implied rejecting religion. Securing social control of religion through violence and political pressure "worked *against* the kingdom of God, because grudging conformity simply is not a joyful life of shared faith, hope, and love."[13] This was why renewed emphasis on *religious freedom* in the Age of Reformations was so significant.

Reviving Religious Freedom

These tragic events of the Age of Reformations that fragmented faith and created conditions favorable to violence prompted spiritual passion and intellectual energy to find solutions. Many knew that faith cannot be forced. But what did that mean in practice? How could one reconcile the duty of ecclesiastical and political leaders to the common good with the freedom of conscience of individuals?

Catholics tried to find political solutions in France. For a long time, they had believed it was the king's responsibility to defend the faith and thereby maintain the political unity of the nation. Their values started to change during the Age of Reformations. As one Frenchman who lived through these changes wrote, "Would you have ever thought in your youth that you would see something so extraordinary that two different religions would be practiced in the same city, and even in the capital of France?"[14] As religious tension mounted in the early 1560s, the French statesman Michel de l'Hôpital argued that government should concern itself with political affairs and not make judgments about doctrine. French society would have to find a way to coexist peacefully despite the presence of two religions.

Few listened. As already discussed, France descended into religious war for decades. However, the compromise that eventually emerged was the Edict of Nantes (1598). This recognized a measure of religious freedom for the French Protestants known as Huguenots. Though it did not please the hard-core Catholics who insisted on loyalty to the traditional idea of "one faith, one law, one king," it served peace by distinguishing between religious identity and civic rights. French Protestants did not gain full equality, but they did secure "safe towns" where they could arm themselves and worship freely. They also obtained bipartisan law courts with equal numbers of Protestant and Catholic judges. This edict was a significant achievement at the time.

Similarly, in the Protestant Netherlands, a sort of compromise emerged in which Anabaptists, Catholics, Lutherans, and Jews could live in the same region under the umbrella of the Dutch Reformed (Calvinist) majority. Catholics often lived near each other and worshipped freely together in their private residences. This kind of religious freedom and private sphere resulted from practical necessity, not from theological or philosophical theories of toleration or religious freedom. Enforcing one kind of religious uniformity across the land would have been simply impossible.

Up Close and Personal:
ST. FRANCIS DE SALES

St. Francis de Sales had many opportunities in life because he was blessed with intelligence, good looks, wealth, and a powerful noble family. He handled these gifts with grace, living a kind, virtuous, and holy life, engendering love from those he met. The death of one of his brothers deepened his conversion, and an education at a Jesuit college prepared him for his future ministry.

John Calvin's reforms in Geneva, Switzerland, began in the 1540s, spreading into the surrounding regions. They effectively created city-states, marrying the government alarmingly close to religion. When Francis was given his post after his ordination, he took on the mission of converting the population of Annecy, a French town twenty miles south of the city of Geneva. The people had been practicing Protestantism for more than fifty years.

Francis focused his efforts on small, diligent works after being offered little welcome. He copied out his sermons and apologetical pamphlets responding to Calvinist doctrine. He reached out to each household by going door to door. If no one answered, or if a door was shut in his face, he slipped his writings under it. These writings were posthumously published as *The Catholic Controversy* and are still in print today. They are reputed as some of the most elegant and effective polemics against Protestantism.

Years of persistence turned the hearts and minds of those he evangelized, and through God's grace, Francis converted thousands. Some say as many as seventy-two thousand people returned to the Catholic faith because of these efforts and later ones when he was installed as bishop of Geneva in 1602 (he still had to reside in Annecy because Catholicism was illegal in Geneva). Francis took inspiration from his friend Charles Borromeo as he cared for his diocese. He was passionate about educating both the clergy and laity and worked hard to keep his diocese very well organized.

Francis wrote for the lay faithful too. His most famous work, *Introduction to the Devout Life*, is a classic today. He also wrote "Treatise on the Love of God" and *Letters of Spiritual Direction*. These spiritual works offer insight on fundamental aspects of lay life and have at their foundation Francis's belief that anyone can and should strive for holiness.

In addition, both Catholic and Protestant thinkers revived the theory of religious freedom in the Age of Reformations in interesting ways. Spanish Catholic writers such as Bartolomé de Las Casas, bishop in southern Mexico, defended the religious freedom of native populations in the Americas against Spanish conquerors who tried to force conversion. He practiced strategies of voluntary conversion based on understanding the faith by the

1530s. In order to defend religious freedom among native populations, Las Casas appealed to natural law and the medieval scholastic principle that even an erroneous conscience binds a person. Theologian David Lantigua argued that the efforts of Las Casas constituted an important step toward the modern commitment to human rights.[15]

Inside Europe, persecuted Protestants and Catholics often appealed to religious freedom. It was Protestant writers, however, who articulated religious freedom most clearly in Europe during the Age of Reformations, such as the Englishman Thomas Helwys (ca. 1575–ca. 1616). He helped start the Baptists, a denomination supporting Radical Protestant ecclesiology concerning the separation of churches from states. Such a division would create a basis for religious freedom, Helwys argued, even for Catholics, whom he otherwise disagreed with profoundly. Like the Catholic Las Casas, Helwys had the clarity of mind to see that religious freedom was a natural endowment for all people and not a concession by the state.[16] Tragically, Helwys died in prison because of the religious persecution of Protestant dissenters under King James I. As head of the Church of England, James believed he had a duty to govern religious affairs. Here again, the overlap of church and state that was supported by political sacralization obscured important truths about the freedom of faith and the dignity of persons.

Catholics like Las Casas and Protestants such as Helwys revived a tradition of religious freedom reaching all the way back to the early centuries of Christianity. Tertullian (ca. AD 155–ca. 240) was the first person in Western civilization to use the phrase "freedom of religion." Constantine enacted religious freedom within the Roman Empire in the Edict of Milan (313). This freedom implied a distinction between Church and state based on Jesus's command "Render therefore to Caesar the things that are Caesar's, and to God the things that are God's" (Mt 22:21). This principle became obscured in the centuries of the Middle Ages when most Christians shared the same church. The emergence of Christian pluralism in the Age of Reformations was regrettable. However, it prompted recovery of the idea of religious freedom. Pluralism did not necessarily imply skepticism or relativism. Individuals and whole communities might very well hold to the truth as they see it while also treating others with different views respectfully. All of this contributed to the paradigm shift toward modern religious sensibilities.

Conclusion

In the Age of Reformations, the painful and exciting transition from medieval to modern times commenced. The religious crisis was brought on by catechetical malfunctions resulting from social and technological changes. In addition, the perception of corruption in the Church and in society changed as utopian ideals of the Renaissance took hold of the imagination of the time. People became more dissatisfied with imperfection. It seemed urgent to eliminate corruption in order to narrow the gap between Christian ideals and ways of life. To close that gap, many kinds of zealous reformers emerged, some of whom wanted to force their visions of godliness on whole populations.

The saints, however, showed great realism and patience in their pursuit of reform. St. Francis de Sales, for example, practiced gentlemanly evangelization through kindness and his teaching style. Saints such as de Sales accepted the call to radical conversion while also recognizing the permanent state of imperfection in the Church and in society. Restraint in front of other peoples' failure and corruption could be difficult for reforming types. The saints knew that we "suffer on account of God's patience," as Pope Benedict XVI said in 2005. "And yet, we need his patience. . . . The world is redeemed by the patience of God. It is destroyed by the impatience of man."[1] The saints held that the Gospel usually acted better as a leaven in society than as a political battering ram. In their nonutopian pursuit of change, the saints held the principle of reform in tension with the principle of apostolic authority in the Church. In that way, they maintained a long-suffering continuity with the Mystical Body of Christ (the Church) that exists in perfection only in heaven.

Notes

Introduction

1. Egidio da Viterbo, "Opening Address," in *The Catholic Reformation: Savonarola to Ignatius Loyola*, ed. John C. Olin, 40–53 (1512; New York: Fordham University Press, 1992), 45, 51, 52.

2. Jerome K. Williams, *True Reformers: Saints of the Catholic Reformation* (Greenwood Village, CO: Augustine Institute, 2017), 10.

3. Yves Congar, *True and False Reform in the Church*, trans. Paul Philibert (1950; Collegeville, MN: Liturgical Press, 2011), 218, 229, 269, 291, 292; Joseph Carey, with Jaroslav Pelikan, "Christianity as an Enfolding Circle," *U.S. News and World Report*, June 26, 1989, 57.

4. Williams, *True Reformers*, 11.

5. Christopher Dawson, "The Frontiers of Necessity: The Social Factor in Religious Belief," *The Tablet*, May 28, 1938, 697.

1. Reform in the Late Middle Ages

1. William Langland, *The Vision of Piers Plowman*, trans. Henry W. Wells (New York: Sheed & Ward, 1935), 11, 13.

2. Catherine of Siena, "Letter to Pope Gregory XI," in *Readings in Church History*, ed. Colman J. Barry, 472–73 (Westminster, MD: Newman Press, 1960), 472.

3. Catherine of Siena, "Letter to Three Italian Cardinals," in *Readings in Church History*, 476–78.

4. Friedrich von Hügel, *The Mystical Element of Religion as Studied in Saint Catherine of Genoa and Her Friends* (1908; London: J. M. Dent & Sons, 1961), 1:44, 51–53, 55, 59, 61, 72, 82.

5. John Hus, "The Treatise on the Church," in *The European Reformations Sourcebook*, ed. Carter Lindberg (Oxford, UK: Blackwell, 2000), 16.

6. James Hannam, "Frequently Asked Questions on the Inquisition," Medieval Science and Philosophy, accessed October 2020, https://jameshannam.com.

7. Ed Condon, "The Spanish Inquisition Was a Moderate Court by the Standards of Its Time," *National Review*, June 27, 2018, accessed October 2020, https://www.nationalreview.com.

8. Henri Daniel-Rops, *The Protestant Reformation*, trans. Audrey Butler (London: J. M. Dent & Sons, 1961), 223.

9. Girolamo Savonarola, "Sermon," in *The Portable Renaissance Reader*, ed. James Bruce Ross and Mary Martin McLaughlin, 644–47 (New York: Penguin Books, 1981), 645.

10. Daniel-Rops, *Protestant Reformation*, 247.

11. Desiderius Erasmus, "Letter to Capito and Letter to Leo X," in *The Portable Renaissance Reader*, ed. James Bruce Ross and Mary Martin McLaughlin, 80–84 (New York: Penguin Books, 1981), 80, 83.

12. Eire, *Reformations*, 65.

13. Eire, *Reformations*, 72.

14. Cyprian, *The Unity of the Catholic Church*, 1st ed., AD 251, in *The Faith of the Early Fathers*, vol. 1, trans. William A. Jurgens (Collegeville, MN: Liturgical Press, 1970), 220–21.

15. Irenaeus, *Against Heresies*, AD 189, 3:3:2, in *The Faith of the Early Fathers*, vol. 1, trans. William A. Jurgens (Collegeville, MN: Liturgical Press, 1970), 90.

16. Damasus, Decree of 382, 3, in *The Faith of the Early Fathers*, vol. 1, trans. William A. Jurgens (Collegeville, MN: Liturgical Press, 1970), 406.

17. Eire, *Reformations*, 72.

18. John Foxe, *The Acts and Monuments*, vol. 3 (1563; London: R. B. Seeley & W. Burnside, 1837), 720.

19. Eamon Duffy, *The Stripping of the Altars: Traditional Religion in England, 1400–1580* (New Haven, CT: Yale University Press, 1992), 532.

20. Langland, *Vision of Piers Plowman*, 17.

21. Walter J. Ong, *Orality and Literacy: The Technologizing of the Word* (New York: Methuen, 1982), 41.

22. Ong, *Orality and Literacy*, 179.

23. Eire, *Reformations*, 84.

24. Duffy, *Stripping of the Altars*, 530, 531.

2. Protestants

1. Eire, *Reformations*, 135.

2. Franz Posset, *The Front-Runner of the Catholic Reformation: The Life and Works of Johann von Staupitz* (Aldershot, UK: Ashgate, 2003), 23.

3. Eire, *Reformations*, 145.

4. Paul Hacker, *The Ego in Faith: Martin Luther and the Origin of Anthropocentric Religion* (1966; Chicago: Franciscan Herald, 1970), 16, 38, 46, 47.

5. Eire, *Reformations*, 148, 149.

6. Posset, *Front-Runner of the Catholic Reformation*, 213, 214, 217.

7. Roland H. Bainton, *Here I Stand: A Life of Martin Luther* (Nashville, TN: Abingdon, 1950), 113.

8. Bainton, *Here I Stand*, 116, 117.

9. James A. Coriden, Thomas J. Green, and Donald E. Heintschel, eds., *The Code of Canon Law* (New York: Paulist, 1985), canon 330, 340; Bainton, *Here I Stand*, 117.

10. Bainton, *Here I Stand*, 119.

11. Erasmus, "To Jodocus Jonas on Luther, May 10, 1521," in *Christian Humanism and the Reformation*, ed. John C. Olin, 150–63 (New York: Harper Torchbooks, 1965), 153, 156, 163.

12. Posset, *Front-Runner of the Catholic Reformation*, 374.

13. Erasmus, "The Axiomata," in *Christian Humanism and the Reformation*, 147.

14. Martin Luther, *Three Treatises* (Philadelphia: Fortress, 1960), 22, 41, 46, 55.

15. Brad S. Gregory, *The Unintended Reformation: How a Religious Revolution Secularized Society* (Cambridge, MA: Belknap/Harvard University Press, 2012), 147; Erasmus, "To Martin Bucer, November 11, 1527," in Lindberg, *The European Reformations Sourcebook*, 263.

16. Luther, *Three Treatises*, 132.

17. Luther, *Three Treatises*, 277, 279, 280, 281, 297.

18. Craig Koslofsky, "Debating the Reformation in Torgau, 1522," in *A Sourcebook of Early Modern European History: Life, Death, and Everything in Between*, ed. Ute Lotz-Heumann, 255–57 (New York: Routledge, 2019).

19. Eire, *Reformations*, qtd. 177. Mark A. Noll, *Turning Points: Decisive Moments in the History of Christianity*, 3rd ed. (Grand Rapids, MI: Baker Academic, 2012), 146.

20. Noll, *Turning Points*, 146.

21. Martin Luther, "An Open Letter on Translating" (1530), Bible Research, June 2003, http://www.bible-researcher.com/luther01.html.

22. Martin Luther, *Everyone's Luther: Prefaces to the Books of the Bible* (2018), 88, 130, http://www.wolfmueller.co/wp-content/uploads/2018/01/Prefaces-to-the-Books-of-the-Bible_with-cover.pdf.

23. Jason Evert, "How to Defend the Deuterocanonicals," *Catholic Answers*, accessed September 2020, https://www.catholic.com/magazine/print-edition/how-to-defend-the-deuterocanonicals.

24. Robert A. Sungenis, *Not by Scripture Alone: A Catholic Critique of the Protestant Doctrine of Sola Scriptura* (Santa Barbara, CA: Queenship, 1997), 329.

25. Erasmus, "Paraclesis," in *Christian Humanism and the Reformation*, 106; Andreas Karlstadt, "On the Removal of the Images," in *The Age of the Reformation*, ed. Roland H. Bainton, 114–15 (1522; Malabar, FL: Krieger, 1956), 114.

26. Eire, *Reformations*, 194.

27. Eire, *Reformations*, 191.

28. Johannes Brenz, *Booklet on the Turk: How Preachers and Laymen Should Conduct Themselves If the Turk Were to Invade Germany* (Wittenberg, 1537), in John W. Bohnstedt, "The Infidel Scourge of God: The Turkish Menace as Seen by German

Pamphleteers of the Reformation Era," *Transactions of the American Philosophical Society* 58, no. 9 (1968): 49.

29. Christopher Rengers, *The 33 Doctors of the Church* (Rockford, IL: TAN Books, 2000), 481.

30. Gregory, *Unintended Reformation*, 98, 101.

31. John Eck, *Enchiridion of Commonplaces of John Eck against Martin Luther and His Followers* (1529; Pittsburgh: Duquesne University, 1976), 2, 8, 9, 11, 12, 25, 46.

32. Eire, *Reformations*, 196; "Müntzer to Frederick the Wise, August 3, 1524," in Lindberg, *The European Reformations Sourcebook*, 89; Thomas Müntzer, "Prague Manifesto," in Lindberg, *The European Reformations Sourcebook*, 84.

33. Müntzer, "Vindication and Refutation," in Lindberg, *The European Reformations Sourcebook*, 90; "Müntzer to the People of Allstedt, April 26 or 27, 1525," in Lindberg, *The European Reformations Sourcebook*, 96–97.

34. Pope Benedict XVI: "In discussing the relationship between the Old and the New Testaments, the Synod also considered those passages in the Bible [such as Deuteronomy 7, cited by Müntzer] which, due to the violence and immorality they occasionally contain, prove obscure and difficult. . . . We should be aware that the correct interpretation of these passages requires a degree of expertise, acquired through a training that interprets the texts in their historical-literary context and within the Christian perspective which has as its ultimate hermeneutical key 'the Gospel and the new commandment of Jesus Christ brought about in the paschal mystery.' I encourage scholars and pastors to help all the faithful to approach these passages through an interpretation which enables their meaning to emerge in the light of the mystery of Christ." See Benedict XVI, *Verbum Domini* (2010), § 42, The Holy See, http://www.vatican.va/content/benedict-xvi/en/apost_exhortations/documents/hf_ben-xvi_exh_20100930_verbum-domini.html.

35. Eire, *Reformations*, 203.

36. Martin Luther, "Against the Robbing and Murdering Hordes of Peasants," in Lindberg, *The European Reformations Sourcebook*, 98.

37. Luther, "An Open Letter on the Harsh Book against the Peasants," in Lindberg, *The European Reformations Sourcebook*, 98.

38. Eire, *Reformations*, 226.

39. Eire, *Reformations*, 229, 230.

40. Eire, *Reformations*, 232.

41. Ulrich Zwingli, "Letter to Matthew Alber Concerning the Lord's Supper, November 16, 1524," in Lindberg, *The European Reformations Sourcebook*, 119; Zwingli, "The Marburg Colloquy and Articles," in Lindberg, *The European Reformations Sourcebook*, 122; Eire, *Reformations*, 233.

42. C. S. Lewis, *Mere Christianity* (San Francisco: HarperSanFrancisco, 1980), 64.

43. Jacopo Sadoleto, "Letter to the Senate and People of Geneva" (1539), Monergism, accessed August 16, 2021, https://www.monergism.com/thethreshold/sdg/calvin_sadolet.html.

44. John Calvin, "Reply by Calvin to Cardinal Sadoleto's Letter" (1539), Monergism, accessed August 16, 2021, https://www.monergism.com/thethreshold/sdg/calvin_sadolet.html.

45. François de Bonivard, "On the Ecclesiastical Polity of Geneva," in Lindberg, *The European Reformations Sourcebook*, 173.

46. Eire, *Reformations*, 308, 310–11.

47. The followers of John Wycliffe (1330–1384) mentioned in chapter 1.

48. Duffy, *Stripping of the Altars*, 80, 87.

49. Henry VIII, *Defence of the Seven Sacraments* (1521), 204, Internet Archive, accessed August 16, 2021, https://archive.org/details/cu31924029398223/page/n7/mode/2up.

50. Williams, *True Reformers*, 49.

51. Williams, *True Reformers*, 55.

52. Thomas More to Margaret Roper, April 17, 1534, Famous Trials, https://famous-trials.com/thomasmore/992-moreinterrogations.

53. Eamon Duffy, *The Voices of Morebath: Reformation and Rebellion in an English Village* (New Haven, CT: Yale University Press, 2001), 134, 140.

54. Duffy, *Stripping of the Altars*, 501.

55. Duffy, *Stripping of the Altars*, 588, 592.

56. Christopher Dawson, *The Dividing of Christendom* (1965; San Francisco: Ignatius, 2008), 35.

57. Alec Ryrie, *Being Protestant in Reformation Britain* (New York: Oxford University Press, 2013), 262, 286.

58. Dawson, *Dividing of Christendom*, 32–34.

3. Catholics

1. François de Sales, *The Catholic Controversy: A Defense of the Faith* (Charlotte, NC: TAN Books, 1989), L, 3.

2. Eire, *Reformations*, 371.

3. Caritas Pirckheimer, *A Journal of the Reformation Years, 1524–1528*, trans. Paul A. MacKenzie (Cambridge, UK: D. S. Brewer, 2006), 73–74.

4. Pirckheimer, *Journal of the Reformation Years*, 74.

5. Pirckheimer, *Journal of the Reformation Years*, 14, 103, 107.

6. Pirckheimer, *Journal of the Reformation Years*, 16.

7. Pirckheimer, *Journal of the Reformation Years*, 16–17.

8. Pirckheimer, *Journal of the Reformation Years*, 125, 134, 135, 136.

9. Pirckheimer, *Journal of the Reformation Years*, 21, 83.

10. Pirckheimer, *Journal of the Reformation Years*, 23–24.

11. Pirckheimer, *Journal of the Reformation Years*, 29, 30.

12. Pirckheimer, *Journal of the Reformation Years*, 32, 33.

13. Pirckheimer, *Journal of the Reformation Years*, 47.

14. Pirckheimer, *Journal of the Reformation Years*, 47, 48, 49.

15. Pirckheimer, *Journal of the Reformation Years*, 89, 90.

16. Pirckheimer, *Journal of the Reformation Years*, 90–91.

17. Pirckheimer, *Journal of the Reformation Years*, 92.

18. Pirckheimer, *Journal of the Reformation Years*, 93, 176.

19. Hermann von Kerssenbrock, *Narrative of the Anabaptist Madness*, trans. Christopher S. Mackay (Leiden, Netherlands: Brill, 2007), 162, 172.

20. Kerssenbrock, *Narrative of the Anabaptist Madness*, 173.

21. Kerssenbrock, *Narrative of the Anabaptist Madness*, 481.

22. James Brodrick, *Saint Ignatius Loyola: The Pilgrim Years, 1491–1538* (San Francisco: Ignatius, 1998), 271, 272.

23. Brodrick, *Saint Ignatius Loyola*, 274.

24. George E. Ganss, ed., *Ignatius of Loyola: The Spiritual Exercises and Selected Works*, Classics of Western Spirituality (New York: Paulist Press, 1991), 430.

25. Ignatius of Loyola, "Rules for Thinking with the Church," in Ganss, *Ignatius of Loyola*, 211, 213.

26. Paul III, "Bull of the Convocation of the Holy Ecumenical Council of Trent," in *Canons and Decrees of the Council of Trent*, ed. H. J. Schroeder, 1–10 (St. Louis, MO: B. Herder, 1941), 6, 7.

27. "Decree Concerning the Manner of Living and Other Matters to Be Observed during the Council," in Schroeder, *Canons and Decrees of the Council of Trent*, 12.

28. "Decree Concerning the Canonical Scriptures," in Schroeder, *Canons and Decrees of the Council of Trent*, 17, 18, 19.

29. John W. O'Malley, *Trent: What Happened at the Council* (Cambridge, MA: Belknap, 2013), 247.

30. Teresa of Ávila, *The Life of Teresa of Jesus*, 82, Carmelite Monks, accessed August 17, 2021, http://www.carmelitemonks.org/Vocation/teresa_life.pdf.

31. O'Malley, *Trent*, 254.

32. Eire, *Reformations*, 384.

33. John R. Cihak, "Introduction: Reform from Within," trans. Ansgar Santogrossi, in *Charles Borromeo: Selected Orations, Homilies and Writings*, ed. John R. Cihak, 1–21 (New York: Bloomsbury, 2017), 3.

34. John XXIII, "Opening Address of the Second Vatican Council," in *The Teachings of the Second Vatican Council* (Westminster, MD: Newman Press, 1966), 4.

35. Charles Borromeo, "Daily Christian Living," in Cihak, *Charles Borromeo*, 163, 164.

36. Ignatius of Loyola, "Formula of the Institute" (1540), 1, Portal to Jesuit Studies, accessed August 17, 2021, https://jesuitportal.bc.edu/research/documents/1540_formula/.

37. John W. O'Malley, *The Jesuits* (Lanham, MD: Rowman & Littlefield, 2014), 17.

38. O'Malley, *The Jesuits*, 7–8.

39. O'Malley, *The Jesuits*, 10, 25; Eire, *Reformations*, 463–64.

40. Eire, *Reformations*, 452.

41. O'Malley, *The Jesuits*, 13.

42. Eire, *Reformations*, 453.

43. O'Malley, *The Jesuits*, 30.

44. O'Malley, *The Jesuits*, 17.

45. Ignatius of Loyola, "To Antonia Araoz" (1551), 2, Portal to Jesuit Studies, accessed August 17, 2021, https://jesuitportal.bc.edu/research/documents/1551_ignatius oninvolvementstudies/; Eire, *Reformations*, 452.

46. Thomas H. Clancy, "Saint Ignatius as Fund-Raiser," *Studies in the Spirituality of Jesuits* 25, no. 1 (January 1993): 1–37.

47. Eire, *Reformations*, 454.

48. Eire, *Reformations*, 454.

49. "Decree Concerning Justification," in Schroeder, *Canons and Decrees of the Council of Trent*, ed. H. J. Schroeder (St. Louis: B. Herder, 1941), 31, 32.

50. "On the Invocation, Veneration, and Relics of Saints, and on Sacred Images," in Schroeder, *Canons and Decrees of the Council of Trent*, 216.

51. Wayne Sattler, *And You Will Find Rest: What God Does in Prayer* (Bismarck, ND: University of Mary Press, 2020), 23–30, 33, 45–46.

52. Elizabeth Lev, *How Catholic Art Saved the Faith: The Triumph of Beauty and Truth in Counter-Reformation Art* (Manchester, NH: Sophia Institute Press, 2018), 21.

53. Lev, *How Catholic Art*, 53.

54. Lev, *How Catholic Art*, 146.

55. Lev, *How Catholic Art*, 144, 181.

4. Consequences

1. St. Teresa of Ávila (1515–1582, Doctor of Prayer), St. Peter Canisius (1521–1597, Doctor of the Catechism), St. Robert Bellarmine (1542–1621, apologist), St. John of the Cross (1542–1591, Doctor of Mystical Theology), St. Lawrence of Brindisi (1559–1619, the Apostolic Doctor), and St. Francis de Sales (1567–1622, the Gentleman Doctor).

2. *From Conflict to Communion: Lutheran-Catholic Common Commemoration of the Reformation in 2017* (Leipzig, Germany: Paderborn, 2013), 7, https://www.lutheran world.org/sites/default/files/From%20Conflict%20to%20Communion%20EN.pdf.

3. Rodney Stark, *Reformation Myths: Five Centuries of Misconceptions and Some Misfortunes* (London: SPCK, 2017), 6, 127, 138, 154, 156.

4. H. Outram Evennett, *The Spirit of the Counter-Reformation* (Notre Dame, IN: University of Notre Dame Press, 1968), 23.

5. Dawson, *Dividing of Christendom*, 31; Gregory, *Unintended Reformation*, 2, 100; Eire, *Reformations*, 585, 756.

6. Eire, *Reformations*, 748.

7. See Joseph T. Stuart, *Rethinking the Enlightenment: Faith in the Age of Reason* (Manchester, NH: Sophia Institute Press, 2020). *Gaudium et Spes* says, "If by the autonomy of earthly affairs we mean that created things and societies themselves enjoy their own laws and values which must be gradually deciphered, put to use, and regulated by men, then it is entirely right to demand that autonomy. . . . Man must respect these [temporal realities] as he isolates them by the appropriate methods of the individual sciences or arts" (36). To the extent that human beings have a religious duty to appreciate and know God's creation, one could even say they have a duty to be secular.

8. Gregory, *Unintended Reformation*, 152.

9. Eire, *Reformations*, 563.

10. Eire, *Reformations*, 601.

11. William T. Cavanaugh, *The Myth of Religious Violence: Secular Ideology and the Roots of Modern Conflict* (New York: Oxford University Press, 2009).

12. Brad S. Gregory, *Salvation at Stake: Christian Martyrdom in Early Modern Europe* (Cambridge, MA: Harvard University Press, 1999), 81, 346.

13. Gregory, *Unintended Reformation*, 160, 161.

14. Robert Louis Wilken, *Liberty in the Things of God: The Christian Origins of Religious Freedom* (New Haven, CT: Yale University Press, 2019), 81.

15. David M. Lantigua, "Faith, Liberty, and the Defense of the Poor: Bishop Las Casas in the History of Human Rights," in *Christianity and Freedom: Historical Perspectives*, ed. Timothy Samuel Shah and Allen D. Hertzke (New York: Cambridge University Press, 2016), 177, 192–99.

16. Wilken, *Liberty in the Things of God*, 140, 180.

Conclusion

1. Benedict XVI, "Inaugural Homily" (2005), The Holy See, http://www.vatican.va/content/benedict-xvi/en/homilies/2005/documents/hf_ben-xvi_hom_20050424_inizio-pontificato.html.

Bibliography

Bainton, Roland H. *Here I Stand: A Life of Martin Luther*. Nashville, TN: Abingdon, 1950.

Benedict XVI. "Inaugural Homily" (2005). The Holy See. http://www.vatican.va/content/benedict-xvi/en/homilies/2005/documents/hf_ben-xvi_hom_20050424_inizio-pontificato.html.

———. *Verbum Domini*. 2010. The Holy See. http://www.vatican.va/content/benedict-xvi/en/apost_exhortations/documents/hf_ben-xvi_exh_20100930_verbum-domini.html.

Bohnstedt, John W. "The Infidel Scourge of God: The Turkish Menace as Seen by German Pamphleteers of the Reformation Era." *Transactions of the American Philosophical Society* 58, no. 9 (1968): 1–58.

Bonivard, François de. "On the Ecclesiastical Polity of Geneva." In *The European Reformations Sourcebook*, edited by Carter Lindberg, 172–73. Oxford, UK: Blackwell, 2000.

Borromeo, Charles. "Daily Christian Living." In *Charles Borromeo: Selected Orations, Homilies and Writings*, edited by John R. Cihak, 163–86. New York: Bloomsbury, 2017.

Brodrick, James. *Saint Ignatius Loyola: The Pilgrim Years, 1491–1538*. San Francisco: Ignatius, 1998.

Calvin, John. "Reply by Calvin to Cardinal Sadoleto's Letter" (1539). Monergism. Accessed August 16, 2021. https://www.monergism.com/thethreshold/sdg/calvin_sadolet.html.

Carey, Joseph, with Jaroslav Pelikan. "Christianity as an Enfolding Circle." *U.S. News and World Report*, June 26, 1989, 57.

Catherine of Siena. "Letter to Pope Gregory XI." In *Readings in Church History*, edited by Colman J. Barry, 472–73. Westminster, MD: Newman Press, 1960.

———. "Letter to Three Italian Cardinals." In *Readings in Church History*, edited by Colman J. Barry, 475–79. Westminster, MD: Newman Press, 1960.

Cavanaugh, William T. *The Myth of Religious Violence: Secular Ideology and the Roots of Modern Conflict*. New York: Oxford University Press, 2009.

Cihak, John R. "Introduction: Reform from Within." Translated by Ansgar Santogrossi. In *Charles Borromeo: Selected Orations, Homilies and Writings*, edited by John R. Cihak, 1–21. New York: Bloomsbury, 2017.

Clancy, Thomas H. "Saint Ignatius as Fund-Raiser." *Studies in the Spirituality of Jesuits* 25, no. 1 (January 1993): 1–37.

Congar, Yves. *True and False Reform in the Church*. Translated by Paul Philibert. 1950; Collegeville, MN: Liturgical Press, 2011.

Coriden, James A., Thomas J. Green, and Donald E. Heintschel, eds. *The Code of Canon Law*. New York: Paulist, 1985.

Cyprian of Carthage. *The Unity of the Catholic Church*. 1st ed., AD 251. In *The Faith of the Early Fathers*, vol. 1, translated by William A. Jurgens, 219–22. Collegeville, MN: Liturgical Press, 1970.

Damasus. Decree of 382. In *The Faith of the Early Fathers*, vol. 1, translated by William A. Jurgens, 404–7. Collegeville, MD: Liturgical Press, 1970.

Daniel-Rops, Henri. *The Protestant Reformation*. Translated by Audrey Butler. London: J. M. Dent & Sons, 1961.

Dawson, Christopher. *The Dividing of Christendom*. 1965; San Francisco: Ignatius, 2008.

———. "The Frontiers of Necessity: The Social Factor in Religious Belief." *The Tablet*, May 28, 1938.

"Decree Concerning Justification." In *Canons and Decrees of the Council of Trent*, edited by H. J. Schroeder, 29–46. St. Louis, MO: B. Herder, 1941.

"Decree Concerning the Canonical Scriptures." In *Canons and Decrees of the Council of Trent*, edited by H. J. Schroeder, 17–20. St. Louis, MO: B. Herder, 1941.

"Decree Concerning the Manner of Living and Other Matters to Be Observed during the Council." In *Canons and Decrees of the Council of Trent*, edited by H. J. Schroeder, 12–14. St. Louis, MO: B. Herder, 1941.

de Sales, François. *The Catholic Controversy: A Defense of the Faith*. Charlotte, NC: TAN Books, 1989.

Duffy, Eamon. *The Stripping of the Altars: Traditional Religion in England, 1400–1580*. New Haven, CT: Yale University Press, 1992.

———. *The Voices of Morebath: Reformation and Rebellion in an English Village*. New Haven, CT: Yale University Press, 2001.

Eck, John. *Enchiridion of Commonplaces of John Eck against Martin Luther and His Followers*. 1529; Pittsburgh: Duquesne University, 1976.

Eire, Carlos M. N. *Reformations: The Early Modern World, 1450–1650*. New Haven, CT: Yale University Press, 2016.

Erasmus, Desiderius. "The Axiomata." In *Christian Humanism and the Reformation*, edited by John C. Olin, 146–49. New York: Harper Torchbooks, 1965.

———. "Paraclesis." In *Christian Humanism and the Reformation*, edited by John C. Olin, 92–106. 1516; New York: Harper Torchbooks, 1965.

———. "Letter to Capito and Letter to Leo X." In *The Portable Renaissance Reader*, edited by James Bruce Ross and Mary Martin McLaughlin, 80–84. New York: Penguin Books, 1981.

———. "To Jodocus Jonas on Luther, May 10, 1521." In *Christian Humanism and the Reformation*, edited by John C. Olin, 150–63. New York: Harper Torchbooks, 1965.

———. "To Martin Bucer, November 11, 1527." In *The European Reformations Sourcebook*, edited by Carter Lindberg, 262–63. Oxford, UK: Blackwell, 2000.

Evennett, H. Outram. *The Spirit of the Counter-Reformation*. Notre Dame, IN: University of Notre Dame Press, 1968.

Foxe, John. *The Acts and Monuments*. Vol. 3, 1563; London: R. B. Seeley & W. Burnside, 1837.

From Conflict to Communion: Lutheran-Catholic Common Commemoration of the Reformation in 2017. Leipzig, Germany: Paderborn, 2013. https://www.lutheranworld.org/sites/default/files/From%20Conflict%20to%20Communion%20EN.pdf.

Ganss, George E., ed. *Ignatius of Loyola: The Spiritual Exercises and Selected Works*. Classics of Western Spirituality. New York: Paulist Press, 1991.

Gregory, Brad S. *Salvation at Stake: Christian Martyrdom in Early Modern Europe*. Cambridge, MA: Harvard University Press, 1999.

———. *The Unintended Reformation: How a Religious Revolution Secularized Society*. Cambridge, MA: Belknap/Harvard University Press, 2012.

Hacker, Paul. *The Ego in Faith: Martin Luther and the Origin of Anthropocentric Religion*. 1966; Chicago: Franciscan Herald, 1970.

Henry VIII. *Defence of the Seven Sacraments*. 1521. Internet Archive. Accessed August 16, 2021. https://archive.org/details/cu31924029398223/page/n7/mode/2up.

Hus, John. "The Treatise on the Church." In *The European Reformations Sourcebook*, edited by Carter Lindberg, 15–16. Oxford, UK: Blackwell, 2000.

Ignatius of Loyola. "Formula of the Institute" (1540). Portal to Jesuit Studies. Accessed August 17, 2021. https://jesuitportal.bc.edu/research/documents/1540_formula/.

———. "Rules for Thinking with the Church." In *Ignatius of Loyola: The Spiritual Exercises and Selected Works*, edited by George E. Ganss. Classics of Western Spirituality, 211–14. New York: Paulist Press, 1991.

———. "To Antonia Araoz" (1551). Portal to Jesuit Studies. Accessed August 17, 2021. https://jesuitportal.bc.edu/research/documents/1551_ignatiusoninvolvementstudies/.

Irenaeus. *Against Heresies*. AD 189. In *The Faith of the Early Fathers*, vol. 1, translated by William A. Jurgens, 84–104. Collegeville, MN: Liturgical Press, 1970.

John XXIII. "Opening Address of the Second Vatican Council." In *The Teachings of the Second Vatican Council*, 1–12. Westminster, MD: Newman Press, 1966.

Karlstadt, Andreas. "On the Removal of the Images." In *The Age of the Reformation*, edited by Roland H. Bainton, 114–15. 1522; Malabar, FL: Krieger, 1956.

Kerssenbrock, Hermann von. *Narrative of the Anabaptist Madness*. Translated by Christopher S. Mackay. Leiden, Netherlands: Brill, 2007.

Koslofsky, Craig. "Debating the Reformation in Torgau, 1522." In *A Sourcebook of Early Modern European History: Life, Death, and Everything in Between*, edited by Ute Lotz-Heumann, 255–57. New York: Routledge, 2019.

Langland, William. *The Vision of Piers Plowman*. Translated by Henry W. Wells. New York: Sheed & Ward, 1935.

Lantigua, David M. "Faith, Liberty, and the Defense of the Poor: Bishop Las Casas in the History of Human Rights." In *Christianity and Freedom: Historical Perspectives*, edited by Timothy Samuel Shah and Allen D. Hertzke, 176–209. New York: Cambridge University Press, 2016.

Lev, Elizabeth. *How Catholic Art Saved the Faith: The Triumph of Beauty and Truth in Counter-Reformation Art*. Manchester, NH: Sophia Institute Press, 2018.

Lewis, C. S. *Mere Christianity*. San Francisco: HarperSanFrancisco, 1980.

Luther, Martin. "Against the Robbing and Murdering Hordes of Peasants." In *The European Reformations Sourcebook*, edited by Carter Lindberg, 97–98. 1525; Oxford, UK: Blackwell, 2000.

———. *Everyone's Luther: Prefaces to the Books of the Bible*. 2018. http://www.wolf-mueller.co/wp-content/uploads/2018/01/Prefaces-to-the-Books-of-the-Bible_with-cover.pdf.

———. "An Open Letter on the Harsh Book against the Peasants." In *The European Reformations Sourcebook*, edited by Carter Lindberg, 98–99. 1525; Oxford, UK: Blackwell, 2000.

———. "An Open Letter on Translating" (1530). Bible Research. Accessed August 18, 2021. http://www.bible-researcher.com/luther01.html.

———. *Three Treatises*. Philadelphia: Fortress, 1960.

Müntzer, Thomas. "Prague Manifesto." In *The European Reformations Sourcebook*, edited by Carter Lindberg, 84–85. 1521; Oxford, UK: Blackwell, 2000

———. "Vindication and Refutation." In *The European Reformations Sourcebook*, edited by Carter Lindberg, 90. 1524; Oxford, UK: Blackwell, 2000.

"Müntzer to Frederick the Wise, August 3, 1524." In *The European Reformations Sourcebook*, edited by Carter Lindberg, 89. Oxford, UK: Blackwell, 2000.

"Müntzer to the People of Allstedt, April 26 or 27, 1525." In *The European Reformations Sourcebook*, edited by Carter Lindberg, 96–97. Oxford, UK: Blackwell, 2000.

Noll, Mark A. *Turning Points: Decisive Moments in the History of Christianity*. 3rd ed. Grand Rapids, MI: Baker Academic, 2012.

O'Malley, John W. *The Jesuits*. Lanham, MD: Rowman & Littlefield, 2014.

———. *Trent: What Happened at the Council*. Cambridge, MA: Belknap, 2013.

Ong, Walter J. *Orality and Literacy: The Technologizing of the Word*. New York: Methuen, 1982.

"On the Invocation, Veneration, and Relics of Saints, and on Sacred Images." In *Canons and Decrees of the Council of Trent*, edited by H. J. Schroeder, 215–17. St. Louis, MO: B. Herder, 1941.

Paul III. "Bull of the Convocation of the Holy Ecumenical Council of Trent." In *Canons and Decrees of the Council of Trent*, edited by H. J. Schroeder, 1–10. St. Louis, MO: B. Herder, 1941.

Pirckheimer, Caritas. *A Journal of the Reformation Years, 1524–1528*. Translated by Paul A. MacKenzie. Cambridge, UK: D. S. Brewer, 2006.

Posset, Franz. *The Front-Runner of the Catholic Reformation: The Life and Works of Johann von Staupitz*. Aldershot, UK: Ashgate, 2003.

Rengers, Christopher. *The 33 Doctors of the Church*. Rockford, IL: TAN Books, 2000.

Ryrie, Alec. *Being Protestant in Reformation Britain*. New York: Oxford University Press, 2013.

Sadoleto, Jacopo. "Letter to the Senate and People of Geneva" (1539). Monergism. Accessed August 16, 2021. https://www.monergism.com/thethreshold/sdg/calvin_sadolet.html.

Sattler, Wayne. *And You Will Find Rest: What God Does in Prayer*. Bismarck, ND: University of Mary Press, 2020.

Savonarola, Girolamo. "Sermon." In *The Portable Renaissance Reader*, edited by James Bruce Ross and Mary Martin McLaughlin, 644–47. New York: Penguin Books, 1981.

Stark, Rodney. *Reformation Myths: Five Centuries of Misconceptions and Some Misfortunes*. London: SPCK, 2017.

Stuart, Joseph T. *Rethinking the Enlightenment: Faith in the Age of Reason*. Manchester, NH: Sophia Institute Press, 2020.

Sungenis, Robert A. *Not by Scripture Alone: A Catholic Critique of the Protestant Doctrine of Sola Scriptura*. Santa Barbara, CA: Queenship, 1997.

Teresa of Ávila. *The Life of Teresa of Jesus*. Carmelite Monks. Accessed August 17, 2021. http://www.carmelitemonks.org/Vocation/teresa_life.pdf.

Viterbo, Egidio da. "Opening Address." In *The Catholic Reformation: Savonarola to Ignatius Loyola*, edited by John C. Olin, 40–53. 1512; New York: Fordham University Press, 1992.

von Hügel, Baron Friedrich. *The Mystical Element of Religion as Studied in Saint Catherine of Genoa and Her Friends*. 1908; London: J. M. Dent & Sons, 1961.

Wilken, Robert Louis. *Liberty in the Things of God: The Christian Origins of Religious Freedom*. New Haven, CT: Yale University Press, 2019.

Williams, Jerome K. *True Reformers: Saints of the Catholic Reformation*. Greenwood Village, CO: Augustine Institute, 2017.

Zwingli, Ulrich. "Letter to Matthew Alber Concerning the Lord's Supper, November 16, 1524." In *The European Reformations Sourcebook*, edited by Carter Lindberg, 119–20. Oxford, UK: Blackwell, 2000.

———. "The Marburg Colloquy and Articles." In *The European Reformations Sourcebook*, edited by Carter Lindberg, 121–23. 1529; Oxford, UK: Blackwell, 2000.

Index

Joseph T. Stuart is an assistant professor of history and a fellow of Catholic studies at the University of Mary. He is the author of *Rethinking the Enlightenment: Faith in the Age of Reason* and *Christopher Dawson: A Cultural Mind in the Age of the Great War*.

He earned an associate's degree from Ferris State University, a bachelor's degree from Franciscan University of Steubenville, a master's degree in modern history from the University of St. Andrews, and a doctorate in modern intellectual history from the University of Edinburgh. Stuart is a land surveyor and an onion farmer, and he coproduced an original play called *North Dakota Voices of the Great War*.

He has been a guest on a variety of Catholic podcasts and radio stations, including Sacred Heart Radio, Ave Maria Radio, Real Presence Radio, and Guadalupe Radio Network. His work has been featured in *Zenit* and *MercatorNet*. He has written for *Prime Matters, The Imaginative Conservative, 360 Review, Homiletic and Pastoral Review*, and *St. Austin Review*.

Stuart lives in Bismarck, North Dakota, with his wife, Barbara, and their three children.

Barbara A. Stuart is a homeschooling mom and social aide who founded and directed a pregnancy resource center in Bismarck, North Dakota.

She earned a bachelor's degree in English from the University of North Dakota and a master's degree in systematic theology from the Christendom Graduate School of Theology. Stuart was a Wilbur Fellow at the Russell Kirk Center for Cultural Renewal in Mecosta, Michigan. Her work has been featured on Real Presence Radio, *Dakota Catholic Action*, and *360 Review*.

Stuart lives in Bismarck with her husband, Joseph, and their three children.

Mike Aquilina is the editor of the Reclaiming Catholic History series and the author of *A History of the Church in 100 Objects, History's Queen*, and *The Church and the Roman Empire (301-490)*.

The Reclaiming
CATHOLIC HISTORY SERIES

The history of the Catholic Church is often clouded by myth, misinformation, and missing pieces. Today there is a renewed interest in recovering the true history of the Church, correcting the record in the wake of centuries of half-truths and noble lies. Books in the Reclaiming Catholic History series, edited by Mike Aquilina and written by leading authors and historians, bring Church history to life, debunking the myths one era at a time.

Titles in the Series Include:

The Early Church

The Church and the Roman Empire

The Church and the Dark Ages

The Church and the Middle Ages

The Church and the Age of Reformations

The Church and the Age of Enlightenment

The Church and the Modern Era

**Look for titles in this series wherever books and eBooks are sold.
Visit avemariapress.com for more information.**